RANDOLPH
CALDECOTT

'Lord of the Nursery'

'Randolph Caldecott'
The Complete Collection of Randolph Caldecott's Contributions to the 'Graphic' (1888)
This portrait was engraved and printed by Edmund Evans.

RANDOLPH CALDECOTT

'Lord of the Nursery'

RODNEY K. ENGEN

ORESKO BOOKS LTD·LONDON

(half title)
'Sketching under Difficulties', Illustration to *Breton Folk. A Tour in Artistic Brittany* (1880)

Caldecott wrote to William Clough in 1878 on his return from visiting Brittany with Henry Blackburn, 'I should have written to you—even from Brittany, the land of cider & sardines—before now, but to confess the truth, the sitting on Inn benches under pretense of studying and sketching the forms of the passerby, for a month is somewhat unhinging to a mind dwelling in a body not over robust.' On the letter he sketched himself as a weary figure draped over a stretcher carried by two Bretons, a sign post stuck in his back (Harvard letter 29 August 1878).

(title page)
'A Modern Orpheus', *Randolph Caldecott Sketches* (1889)

During his early struggles in London Caldecott wrote to a friend, '....for I am busy—not accumulating wealth, oh John, but wearing my life away in pursuit of fame & fortune. Gaze on this, shed a tear, & take another egg [accompanied with a sketch of the devil grasping bags of gold and guineas, a classical maiden with ribbon marked "Fame" being chased by a wiry young man]. I have four powerful blisters on my right hand now—Pheugh!' (Harvard letter 21 September 1873).

ACKNOWLEDGEMENTS

I would like to express my appreciation for the assistance of the following individuals in the preparation of this book: Mr. Michael Regan, Exhibitions Officer, Whitworth Art Gallery and the staff of the gallery's print room for photographs and cataloguing information; Mr. L. G. Lovell, Director of the City Art Gallery, Manchester; Mr. Julian Treuherz and his assistant at the City Art Gallery for photographs, biographical information and for their enthusiasm which will hopefully lead to a major exhibition of Caldecott's work; to the Keeper of Fine Art at Chester for cataloguing information; to Mr. A. J. Chapman, assistant manager, Williams and Glyn's Bank, Manchester, for his eager assistance in tracing Caldecott's early banking career; to Miss Martha Eliza Shaw of the Houghton Library, Harvard University for prompt delivery of photographs, letters, and cataloguing information; to Elizabeth Billington for advice as to the location of Caldecott's works in America; to the staff of the Victoria and Albert Museum print room and library for permission to photograph selected works; to the staff of the British Library, the Swiss Cottage Reference Library, London Borough of Camden; to Messrs. Phillips and Sotheby's for cataloguing information, and to Michael Smith for research assistance.

R.K.E.
London 1976

First published in Great Britain by
Oresko Books Ltd., 30 Notting Hill Gate, London W11

ISBN 0 905368 02 9 (cloth) ISBN 0 905368 03 7 (paper)
Copyright © Oresko Books Ltd. 1976

Printed in Great Britain by
Burgess & Son (Abingdon) Ltd., Abingdon, Oxfordshire

Contents

'Fox-hunting in America—A Fancy', 'American Facts and Fancies II', *Graphic,* February-June 1886

This picture carried the following caption:
'The most prominent features of the landscape as seen from the train between New York and Washington are the huge advertisements in white letters painted upon black wooden barns and workshops, and upon long black hoardings specially set up in the fields within view of the railway, but not close to the line. I hear that even natural rocks are made to bear these marks of commercial enterprise. As I was told that there were plenty of packs of foxhounds in the Eastern States, I could not help having a vision of a hunting scene, and I here give a sketch of it as it appeared to my mind's eye.'

Randolph Caldecott

'The Genius of Randolph Caldecott will stand for all time. Caldecott is lord of the nursery.
No one ever yet approached him. He is supreme. Every nursery—every child's bookshelf that
does not contain his Picture Books is poor indeed.'

Book jacket, *R. Caldecott's Picture Book* No. 4, c.1906

THE ILLUSTRATIONS, PAINTINGS and sculpture of Randolph Caldecott, who lived a brief forty years during the height of Victorian aestheticism, represented a unique form of escapism: an escape to the quiet country lanes of eighteenth-century England, where ladies in crinolines and rotund squires presided over vast estates, where scarlet-jacketed huntsmen sent their horses leaping over a countryside uninhabited by locomotives and unmarred by the smoke stacks of a distant factory. Caldecott's John Gilpin or the coachman in *Old Christmas* raced through the nursery, into the parlours of late Victorian England and across the ocean to the Continent to charm both children and adults throughout the English-speaking, and, indeed, the French-speaking worlds.

But Caldecott's world was not entirely an historic one, for he recorded the lives and attitudes of his contemporaries wherever he travelled. He drew the English tourist bobbing in the Channel at Trouville, groups of carefully dressed young girls promenading the seafront at Menton, or the dejected gambling failure sitting in a casino at Cannes. His pictures encouraged travel to Italy, northern France, the Riviera and even America at a time when Oscar Wilde was preaching the tenets of self-conscious living at home.

Caldecott's style was unique without being forced or determinedly novel. His illustrations reached the drawing rooms depicted in *Punch* by his friend and fellow illustrator, George Du Maurier, and filled the nurseries with a freshness and a wholesome quality which went beyond the forced lessons of any religious tract society. His style was direct, clean and effective, while his drawing set standards for economy of line, which Walter Crane felt was the basis of all good design and which Paul Gauguin, an ardent admirer of Caldecott's work, claimed 'was the true spirit of drawing'.

Randolph Caldecott was born at Bridge Street in the walled village of Chester, Cheshire on 22 March 1846, six days before the birth of his future rival Kate Greenaway and a year after Walter Crane. The son of an accountant 'in good standing', he attended King Henry VII School, where, under James Harris, he was elected head boy. Although his father discouraged his early artistic efforts, Caldecott wandered through the local countryside, sketching from nature and from the age of six he was carving wooden animals, modelling in clay and painting. Arthur Locker, editor of the *Graphic*, to which Caldecott contributed some of his best illustrations from 1872, wrote of the young man's studies:

He must have begun, moreover, at a very early age, for just after Caldecott's death, the writer of these lines picked up at a bookstall a ragged old Virgil which had belonged to the future illustrator of Washington Irving when a Chester schoolboy, and which was adorned with sundry pen and ink sketches, exhibiting, however it must be frankly said, no more special talent than is shown by scores of lads who have a turn for drawing.... It was only gradually that Caldecott discovered his real vocation.[1]

At the age of fifteen Caldecott moved to Whitchurch, Shropshire, where he took a job as a clerk in the Whitchurch Ellesmere Bank, also accepting an agency for life insurance, where he remained for six years from 1861 to 1867. His work was not difficult so he could spend much of his 'off-time' drawing in the countryside, where he lived in an old farmhouse two miles outside the villlage. Here he walked or took his favourite vehicle, the country gig, to call on friends, to go fishing, shooting, to meets of the hounds, to visit markets and cattle fairs, experiences which he later used to illustrate his famous Picture Books. During his first year at Whitchurch, Caldecott saw his first illustration published in the *Illustrated London News* (cf. appendix). This must have pleased the young artist who, by this time, was described by a friend as having an engaging appearance and manner, attributes which proved important when he later attempted to break into London's artistic circles.

We who knew him can well understand how welcome he must have been in many a cottage, farm and hall. The handsome lad carried his own recommendation. With light brown hair falling with a ripple over his brow, blue-grey eyes shaded by long lashes, sweet and mobile mouth, tall and well made, he joined to these physical advantages a gay humour and a charming disposition. No wonder then that he was a general favourite.[2]

On 24 December 1866 Caldecott met William Langton, managing director of the Manchester and Salford bank, now Williams and Glyn's Bank, presumably to apply for a post as clerk.[3] He was accepted and moved to Manchester in 1867 to begin work in a city where his artistic ambitions could materialise. The mere size and diversity of Manchester must have seemed overwhelming at first to the young man after six years in a sleepy Shropshire village, although he may have visited Manchester on earlier occasions. Indeed, throughout his life Caldecott visited as many new cities, and, later, countries on the Continent, as possible, recording his experiences for book and periodical illustrations. William Clough described his new friend's youthful curiosity during the period they were both employed at the bank.

Caldecott used to wander about the bustling, murky streets of Manchester, sometimes finding himself in queer out-of-the-way quarters often coming across an odd character, curious bits of antiquity and the like. Whenever the chance came he made short excursions into the adjacent country, and long walks which were never purposeless....Whilst in this city so close was his application to the art that he loved that on several occasions he spent the whole night drawing.[4]

Manchester was undeniably one of the wealthiest cities in England when Caldecott arrived. A local paper described the county in 1870 with the words 'In Lancashire, we are rich beyond the dreams of avarice'.[5] In addition to the growing population and land area the city contained two of England's oldest schools, the oldest free library, a natural history society, twelve local newspapers, eight founded in the 1860s, four in the 1870s, and numerous businessmen's clubs which lent money to the arts.

The Manchester and Salford Bank, for which Caldecott worked, was a prestigious institution, established in 1836, and, from 1862, housed in an impressive new building at 38 Mosley Street designed by Edward Walters in the Renaissance style. The young artist must have enjoyed the congenial nature of his employer, William Langton, a noted arts patron, whom his obituary described as 'artist, antiquary and linguist'.[6] Indeed, while working at the bank, Caldecott became known for his charming practical jokes and jovial nature. Seated behind one of the numerous dark wood desks in the bank's great hall, under an encrusted plaster-work ceiling supported by columns capped in gold, he would watch the customers enter through the barrel-vaulted entry and make quick sketches of them on envelopes and odd pieces of stationery. These informal efforts formed the basis for Caldecott's habit of recording life around him, a technique he was to use while serving as a special reporter for several London periodicals. In a sketch-book prepared by William Clough (now owned by the Victoria and Albert Museum, London), forty-one of these sketches indicate the wide range of the young Caldecott's interests: a gentleman in stove-pipe trousers and tall hat was placed next to a donkey's head; sheets of portrait heads on envelope edges recorded elements of character; a miserly-looking old man was positioned near a grotesque; landscapes of Whitchurch, dated 1870, and Ellesmere were drawn with a delicate etcher's line that foreshadowed his later travelogue sketches; two cartoon-like figures labelled 'Hermit' and 'Rake' were followed by a fine pen and ink drawing, 'Ancient Welsh Bard'.[7] Indeed, in a letter to William Clough in 1885, on the death of an old banking associate, Caldecott confessed, 'As for me, I am sure I must have caused him moments of dissatisfaction and uneasiness. There was seldom visible in me any steady sober respect for the work of the bank.'[8]

Caldecott became an evening student at the Manchester School of Art, an influential institution where, in later years (1893-1896), his friend and rival illustrator Walter Crane was to serve as Director of Design. The school's policies were explained by Caldecott's friend Alfred Derbyshire, a fellow member of the Brasenose Club and art school student in the 1850s.

Looking back to the days of his mastership [J. A. Hammersley], it seems to me that Schools of Art were very inferior places for study and artistic advancement compared with similar institutions which flourished all over the country at the close of the nineteenth century. They were certainly not calculated to make painters of pictures; the curriculum of study was based upon the idea that line-drawing was favourable to design, as applied to the manufactures carried on in such a commercial centre as Manchester. Those Schools of Art were originally called Schools of Design.[9]

Perhaps Caldecott developed his skilful linear dexterity from such a curriculum, although he was largely a self-taught artist and attended two art schools for only brief periods in his career.

He remained in Manchester for five years from 1867 to 1872, working continuously at his art which he now felt to be his chosen profession. He began to mix in the city's artistic circles and to make friends with local artists including the portrait sculptor Matthew Noble (1818-1876), who had just completed the monumental statue of the Prince Consort (1867) for Albert Square. Caldecott eased the limitations of his job at the bank by joining one of the city's businessmen's clubs, the Brasenose Club, described by a sour M.P. as 'the Abiding Place of Genius and the Home of Vice'. The club's historian recalled that 'In the early years of the Club's life might be seen poor Randolph Caldecott, frail and delicate-looking, but full of dry humour.'[10] Caldecott's membership was to prove an important step towards the advancement of his artistic career.

The Brasenose Club, founded in 1869, was one of Manchester's major centres of artistic life. The club's preamble stated its aim 'to promote the association of gentlemen of literary, scientific, or artistic professions, pursuits or tastes', and among the original members were Sir Charles Hallé, Alfred Waterhouse, RA, Edwin Waugh, the Lancashire poet whose works Caldecott later illustrated (cf. appendix), the actor Charles Calvert and several local journalists and art school administrators. In the club's commonroom Caldecott learned about the difficulties of a journalist's life, a spur to his interest in an early career as an illustrator-reporter. For an ambitious bachelor in his early twenties seeking new experiences to turn into drawings, this club must have been just the place to make artistic and social contacts. The club walls were lined with the works of its artist members, stacks of newspapers on the tables contained reviews of performances of its actor members. In a glittering statement of self-congratulatory prose, one member described the club's role, when interviewed in a local paper.

A club like the Brasenose helps to fix a standard of intellect and manners beneath which no man may fall without loss of caste. It subordinates brass to brains, and pays tribute to the true Caesar. The Brasenose should have no duality of worship. It should be monotheism, and the god of its idolatry should be and I think it is—Genius.[11]

The club also organised several artistic events, including an exhibition of mezzotints after Reynolds (1874), the works of J. D. Watson (1877) and of Joseph Knight (1878) and a loan collection of Caldecott's works (1888), two years after his death.

Caldecott's artistic career began to grow—his published work while in Manchester included illustrations to the Will o' the Wisp, a local serio-comic paper (cf. appendix), and two full-page comic series in The Sphinx, another short-lived local paper (cf. appendix). They were executed in a style borrowed from John Leech (in which connection it is interesting to note that two of Leech's sketches were exhibited posthumously next to Caldecott's works at the Dudley Gallery, London, in 1872). These sketchy pen and ink drawings were crude and relied on shaded backgrounds to hide figures drawn out of proportion; still a subtle humour was evident in the single lines of each character's face. As early efforts they provide a rather tentative glimpse at Caldecott's youthful potential while serving as evidence of the magazine's promise to include from this number on 'illustrations comprising portraits, views, architectural drawings, works of art and social and Humorous Sketches. . . . executed by competent artists.'[12] Unfortunately further examples of Caldecott's work were not included in forthcoming issues. He also exhibited his first work in Manchester, a hunting frieze painted white on brown paper and entitled 'At the Wrong End of the Wood', which appeared at the Royal Manchester Institution in 1869, near works by such notable artists as G. F. Watts, E. M. Ward and J. Archer. But the lure of the London art world, represented by these artists, beckoned young Caldecott. Only in London could an aspiring illustrator find real work and a promising future.

London in the 1870s was a mecca for artists; the successful expatriot Frenchmen Alphonse Legros and sculptor Jules Dalou, who later became Caldecott's modelling instructor, had both fled France as a result of the Paris Commune of 1870 and sought refuge in London, where opportunities for young artists were numerous. Indeed, a number of artists from Manchester moved to London, including J. D. Watson and Thomas Armstrong. It was probably not surprising then that the young Caldecott set off to visit London in May 1870, with a letter of introduction to Armstrong from William Slagg, the brother of a portrait painter. Caldecott, 'determined to make a first experiment with an editor',[13] met the gracious and influential Thomas Armstrong, who, perhaps, glimpsing a reflection of his own early attempts to leave Manchester for London, secured Caldecott's introduction to Mark Lemon, editor of *Punch*. Lemon examined a small drawing on wood and a book of sketches, 'Fancies of a Wedding', presumably similar in style to *The Sphinx* drawings. The sketch on wood was accepted and the book of drawings retained, but Caldecott recalled later that 'From that day to this, I have never seen either sketch or book. The first never appeared, inspite of the promise, and the second has probably been lost.'[14] However his career as an illustrator for London periodicals had begun and he returned to Manchester to work from 1870 through 1871, posting great numbers of drawings to London, 'some of which,' in the words of one editor, 'have never been exceeded for humour and expression in a few lines.'[15]

Caldecott's diary for 3 November 1870 reveals an important development in his career. 'Some drawings which I left with A. [Armstrong] have been shown, accompanied by a letter from Du Maurier, to a man [Henry Blackburn] on *London Society*. Must wait a bit and go on working—especially studying horses A. said.'[16] Obviously, Caldecott's work made an impression on Blackburn, for his first drawing for *London Society* appeared in February 1871 (cf. appendix).

London Society was a popular, illustrated shilling periodical founded in 1862 by James Hogg, 'aiming to be a "smart" and topical magazine, with the mood of the hour reflected in its pages.'[17] Caldecott's drawings were in good company here, for the magazine's other artists included John Gilbert, George Du Maurier, John Everett Millais,

'Could not draw a lady!'

Walter Crane, Edward Poynter, J. D. Watson and William Small. Caldecott's own work, however, aroused controversy in several instances.

The sketches were made always from his own point of view, and some were so grotesque, and hit so hard at aristocracy, that they were found inappropriate to a fashionable magazine!—one especially of Hyde Park in the afternoon called 'Sons of Toil', had to be declined by the Editor with real regret.[18]

In addition a letter to the editor in 1872 claimed that Caldecott was not capable of drawing a lady. This criticism evidently affected the young artist, who parodied the remark in a letter sent to a friend with a sketch of himself holding up a chalice marked 'inspiration' and seated before an easel and a lady model.[19]

Henry Blackburn played an important role in Caldecott's life: first as the influential editor of *London Society*, noted travel writer, publisher of *Academy Notes* (a series of gallery guides illustrated with sketches by the artists whose works were exhibited), Caldecott's friend and later as his biographer. Blackburn selected most of the young man's drawings for publication and gave the first and most popular, 'A Debating Society', to the master wood-engraver James D. Cooper, with whom Caldecott shared his first successful book commission five years later.

Caldecott's work for *London Society* consisted, primarily, of incidental page fillers, often without a real connection to the text. His sketches to the story 'The Two Trombones' by F. Robson represented a first attempt at illustrating a specific story. The subtle humour which charged these early efforts compensated, perhaps, for the limited technical skill they betrayed. Blackburn's major problem, however, in dealing with Caldecott's contributions to the magazine came in making a selection from the enormous number of drawings the artist submitted by post. 'What to do with all the material sent? was the question in 1871,' Blackburn reminisced.[20]

Caldecott was so encouraged by the sale of a small oil painting and watercolour in the early part of 1872 that at the age of twenty-six, buoyed by his friends' encouragement and advice, he left his £100-a-year job as a bank clerk and moved to London for the uncertain career of an illustrator. 'I had the money in my pocket sufficient to keep me for a year or so, and was hopeful that during that time my powers would be developed and my style improved so much that I should find plenty of work.'[21]

The illustrated letter from Court shows handwritten text:

> Being in Westminster Hall the other day, I stepped into the Court of Probate, and heard part of the famous case of Bulmer v. Shuker. The apparently careless, but really clever, cross-examination of the plaintiff's principal witness by the Solicitor General (who wears a very untidy wig — by the way) filled me with awe & admiration for that great lawyer until Mr Serjeant Ballantine rose and said he didn't care &

Illustrated letter from Court, *Randolph Caldecott Sketches* (1889)

London represented an important step in Caldecott's career, as he wrote to an anonymous Manchester friend on 21 July 1872:

London is of course the proper place for a young man, for seeing the manners and customs of society, and for getting a living in some of the less frequent grooves of human labour, but for a residence give me a rural or marine retreat. I sigh for some 'cool sequestered spot'; the world forgetting, by the world forgot![22]

Attached to the letter was a sketch of him sitting in the bath.

Caldecott's early days in London were spent wandering in search of material to fill his sketchbook, after which he would return to his small studio flat at 46 Great Russell Street, opposite the British Museum. A journalist described his routine:

He would stroll down to the Houses of Parliament and sketch the members, and the groups that congregated about the Law Courts—judges, barristers, witnesses, were all one to him. If there was a fashionable wedding, a meeting at Exeter Hall, a great public gathering of any kind, a new piece at the theatre, he made one of the party. He frequented the Parks and roamed about the streets in the same way that he had roamed about the Shropshire lanes, and neither pencil nor imagination was ever at rest.[23]

'Drawing from familiar objects'

The early days of 1872 were filled by completing drawings for *London Society,* studying from 16 April to 29 June at the Slade School under Edward Poynter, who later became an honorary member of the Manchester Brasenose Club, and planning paintings of birds and animals. Caldecott's letters at this time show an optimism tinged with loneliness. In one he portrayed himself before a table of empty wine bottles as he lashed out at those critics who despised the influence of drink as a damaging influence on the artist, while in another, written on New Year's Eve, the handwriting is barely legible, obviously due to the influence of alcohol.[24]

As his work became known his friends grew in number. His willingness to learn and develop his talent must have endeared him to many artists, whom he could soon count as his friends. George Du Maurier, John Leech's successor as editor of *Punch,* praised Caldecott's work and provided an early boost to his career, as did the comic illustrator Charles Keene and the neoclassical painter Albert Moore. In the autumn of 1873 Caldecott entered into an agreement with the French expatriot sculptor Jules Dalou (1838-1902) whereby he would give English lessons in return for instruction in modelling clay. Dalou, then an influential artist whose friends included Edward Poynter, Frederick Leighton and Lawrence Alma-Tadema, for whom he had executed portrait medallions, had an important impact on the young Caldecott. He would visit Dalou in his Chelsea studio and work from clay models which formed the basis for his later bas-reliefs and statuettes (cf. appendix).

Most important of all, however, was his relationship with Thomas Armstrong, his closest London friend, who served as an artistic adviser, providing a studio and work, and acted as a brother to the lonely young artist, who greatly valued Armstrong's counsel. His early diary is filled with instructions which he followed religiously: 'A. [Armstrong] urged me to prepare caricatures of people well-known' [presumably as practice for periodical work] (8 June 1872); 'A. came to see my wax models; liked them, said I must do something further' (24 April 1873); 'At Armstrong's all day. Began to paint pigeons on canvas panel. Looking at pigeons in the British Museum quadrangle' (10 April 1874).[25]

Caldecott became a member of a social group in the London art world strongly reminiscent of the Paris Armstrong knew and which was portrayed in George Du Maurier's novel, *Trilby.* In addition to Du Maurier and Armstrong, its members included L. M. Lamont, Edward Poynter, and Walter Crane, to whose son, Lionel,

Armstrong was a godfather. Lamont described the pattern.

Armstrong and Caldecott met almost daily and the dining circle at Greliche's, a restaurant just off Oxford Street, near Poland Street, comprised, besides Lamont, Mr. Joseph Wallis, architect, Albert Moore, [William] Allingham, and occasionally Mr. Henry Blackburn....[26]

Armstrong delegated work to Caldecott from his own decorative interior commissions. Returning (c. 1873) from a second visit to Italy to work with W. E. Nesfield on the interior of Henry Renshaw's Bank Hall, near Chapel-en-le-Frith, Derbyshire, Armstrong undertook the dining room decorations, collaborating with Caldecott, who painted a series of birds in oil on large six foot wall panels. These, framed in oak mouldings, were subsequently exhibited at Deschamp's Gallery and the Derbyshire commission was followed in 1875 by work at Broome Hall, Holmewood.

It is interesting to speculate that Caldecott developed an interest in art history and literature, particularly that of the eighteenth century, from his association with Armstrong. Certainly, the Georgian era is closely associated with many of his most famous book illustrations, and Lamont's description of Armstrong's keen interest in the period could apply equally well to Caldecott's work.

For surrounding, for music, for costume, Armstrong has been apt to turn towards England of the eighteenth century, as who would not turn if such as care for simple refinement and reserve in outward things, for a natural and demure inventiveness in the accessories of life that is full of an irrepressible charm?[27]

Caldecott's first commissioned book illustrations, however, grew out of a Continental holiday rather than from his affinity with eighteenth-century England. The diary entry for 20 August 1872 records, 'To Rotterdam, Harzburg, &c. to join Mr. and Mrs. B. [Blackburn] in the Harz Mountains' and the result of this expedition was twenty-four sketches for Henry Blackburn's *The Harz Mountains: A Tour in the Toy Country* (1873). Caldecott's contributions were published alongside thirteen illustrations by other artists, making the book, predictably, a rather irregular mixture. Caldecott's selection of scenes was purely abitrary, often tinged with the grotesque as in 'Hexen Tanzplatz', which depicts a dance of witches, while his landscapes stressed individuals rather than countryside, in order to capture what he called 'the life of the place'. Armed with a Baedeker's guide and a dialogue book, Caldecott tramped through the Harz Mountains, allowing his pen to record whatever he encountered.

Following the London publication of *Harz Mountains*, Blackburn took a scrapbook of Caldecott's proofs with him to New York, where twenty-two of the drawings were published in an eighteen-page excerpt from the book in *Harper's New Monthly Magazine* (June 1873) (cf. appendix). Additional illustrations from the book were reproduced in the London *Graphic* for October 1872, marking the beginning of Caldecott's long association with that periodical.

Caldecott's next commission was recorded in his diary during January 1873, '[I] made six illustrations for Frank Mildmay by Florence Marryat'. This work, which appeared in 1873 with six full-page illustrations, was the reprinted edition of Captain Marryat's classic, *The Naval Officer or Scenes and Adventures in the Life of Frank Mildmay,* originally published in three volumes in 1829.

This commission's main importance was in marking Caldecott's earliest association with the publisher George Routledge and the engraver Edmund Evans, the men who in five years collaborated with him on the Picture Books which expanded his reputation to worldwide proportions.

It must be remembered that throughout his career Caldecott was plagued with chronic ill health. An early attack of rheumatic fever had weakened his heart, and although he had the will to be constantly active and longed to walk or ride through the countryside, this disability often limited such activities. Later, when still in his thirties, he suffered from gastritis which eventually proved fatal. More than once his health proved an obstacle to his work, as he wrote to William Etches on 28 March 1873 from London.

About the middle of February I went down into the country to make some studies and sketches, and remained for more than a month. Had several smart attacks on the heart, a little wounded once, causing that machine to go up and down like a lamb's tail when its owner is partaking of the nourishment provided by bounteous Nature.[28]

In spite of his ill health Caldecott bore the strain of work as a 'special reporter' from the middle of 1873 until 1875, providing illustrations to the New York *Daily Graphic*, the London *Pictorial World* and, later, the London *Graphic*. This position could sap the strength of even the healthiest of artists, but Caldecott undoubtedly knew of the urgency to reach a destination and record a story before a deadline that his colleague Harry Furniss, 'special reporter' for the *Illustrated London News*, described in his autobiography.

I sat up all night and drew a page on wood, ready for engraving, and sent it off by the first train in the morning. It was in the press before my rival's rough notes left Liverpool. One would hardly think, to see candles stuck in my boots, that the hotel was the Old Adelphi. I trust the 'special' of the future will find the electric light, or a better supply of bedroom candlesticks. All day again sketching, and all night hard at work, burning the midnight oil (I was nearly writing books).... And after another day of this kind of thing, I reached home without having had an hour's sleep. Oh! a 'special's' life is not a happy one.[29]

One of Caldecott's assignments as the 'London artistic correspondent' to the New York *Daily Graphic* was to accompany Henry Blackburn to the Universal Exhibition of Arts and Industry which opened on 1 May 1873 in Vienna. He must have relished this second visit to the Continent, and sent back numerous travel sketches made en route and at the exhibition, which was housed in a palatial iron and glass hall, similar to the Crystal Palace of 1851, with a central rotunda under which were displayed examples of manufactured goods from all over the world. To these travel sketches Caldecott added portraits of American visitors at a Fourth of July celebration, a sketch of a Viennese dog, and, his most successful drawing of a tram ride, 'Off to the Exhibition'.

These illustrations were important in being amongst the first reproduced directly from pen and ink drawings by photo-lithography, a process which not only eliminated the time-consuming intervention of the wood-engraver, but also maintained the spontaneous quality of the original sketches. Indeed the *Daily Graphic* had earned the admiration of the English press since its establishment in 1873, for it marked the beginning of the reassessment of illustrated periodicals soon to be dominated by the photo-engraving processes of the 1880s. Henry Blackburn was a major figure in this reassessment. In a lecture, 'The Art of

'The Morning Walk', published in *The Pictorial World*, July 1874

Popular Illustration', delivered to the London Society of Art (for which Caldecott provided large brush illustrations, 7′ × 5′, to stress key points), he used the success of the New York *Daily Graphic* to emphasise the need for an illustrated London daily newspaper with unparalleled quality reproductions. He described the *Daily Graphic's* working schedule which provided insight into the working conditions of its artists, including Caldecott.

The illustrations are printed from six steam presses, generally between the hours of 9 and 12 in the morning, and have to be drawn often at the dead of night. There were six artists on the staff when I was in New York, with varying powers of skill, imagination, and endurance; one I know has survived, for he is in this room. The paper was published at two in the afternoon, and between that hour and six there were spread over the city of New York the most remarkable illustrations of events it has ever been my lot to witness.[30]

Caldecott's work for the paper took him to lectures—he drew a portrait of Mark Twain lecturing in London in 1873—and in his spare moments he made life studies at the London Zoological Gardens or from birds at Armstrong's studio.

In spite of the fact that his talents suited journalistic work, Caldecott never adjusted to the journalist's rapid pace of life, neither on *Punch*, the London *Graphic*, nor the new *Pictorial World* could he be engaged as a regular contributor. He would, however, do almost any work to assist a friend, especially Henry Blackburn who in 1874 was engaged as art editor to a new illustrated periodical,

The Pictorial World: An Illustrated Weekly Newspaper (published from 7 March 1874 and running for 478 numbers to 9 July 1892). The first number stated its intentions 'to present to the great middle-class of England, and of all English-speaking countries, a weekly illustrated record of passing events, which shall be pure in tone, amusing in its contents and graceful to the eye' and presented the interesting proposal that 'In *The Pictorial World* authors and artists will work together—each will inspire the other.'[31] Caldecott's illustrations for the first number were scenes from important public events—'The Close of the Tichborne Trial' and 'Sketches of the Recent Elections' (cf. appendix), reproduced by new production methods such as Dawson's New Etching Process. Other contributions were copied from his large studio paintings and proved the most successful, such as 'Coursing' and 'Morning Walk'. He nevertheless refused a regular position on the paper at £10 and ten shillings a week.

The year 1874 was crucial to Caldecott's early career, the period when Caldecott formulated the style which was to make his reputation. His diary for 23 January 1874 records, 'J. Cooper, engraver, came and proposed to illustrate with seventy or eighty sketches, Washington Irving's *Sketch Book*. Went all through it and left me to consider. I like the idea.' The result was *Old Christmas* (1876), with 120 illustrations by Caldecott, completed at Henry Blackburn's cottage, Farnham Royal, Buckinghamshire, where a small shed, the 'loose box', adjoining the stable, had been converted into a studio. Here Caldecott spent the summers of 1872, 1873 and 1874, enthusiastically drawing the landscape, the local gardener, the groom and the parish clerk, all included in *Old Christmas*.

The artist was twenty-nine when Macmillan & Co. published *Old Christmas*. Caldecott's second commission for Macmillan (in the previous year he had contributed eight illustrations to Louisa Morgan's *Baron Bruno*). *Old Christmas*, was a selection from *The Sketch Book of Geoffrey Crayon*, Washington Irving's observations in England from 1805 to 1815, originally published in three illustrated volumes in 1820. The 1875 version extracted five chapters with the plea in the preface, 'Their [Caldecott and Cooper] primary idea was to carry out the principle of the *Sketch Book*, by incorporating the designs with the text. Throughout they have worked together and *con amore*. With what success the public must decide.'

The public's decision was unanimously in favour of the volume which Macmillan printed in October 1875, reprinted with slight alterations in December 1875 and reprinted again in 1877. *The Pictorial World* reviewer claimed, 'the book is intended for the fireside of the reading folks in all classes....so pleased are we with the designs, which exceed a hundred in number, that we have transferred them to our pages.'[32] The paper's art editor made the extravagant claim, 'Surely it has seldom happened in the history of illustration that an author should be so very closely followed—if not overtaken—by his illustrator.'[33]

The book's illustrations varied from full-page engravings on buff-tinted paper to slight sketched character vignettes cut into the body text, an idea suggested by J. D. Cooper. Their style was still erratic, often changing within the space of two pages, for instance on pages 96-7, the plates were presumably drawn months apart from each other. The overall effect, however, was a subtle charm which recreated the England of the eighteenth century.

'The Cottage, Farnham Royal'

Illustration to *Old Christmas* (1876)

'The Stage Coach', illustration to *Old Christmas* (1876)

Caldecott had carefully studied and retained Washington Irving's observations while applying to the figures and animals his own formula for making them appear life-like. Surprisingly, before Macmillan decided to publish the book, it was rejected by several publishers; one considered the illustrations 'inartistic, flippant, vulgar and unworthy of the author of Old Christmas'.[34]

Old Christmas was followed by its sequel, *Bracebridge Hall* (1877), which promised to be 'illustrated by the same able pencil, but condensed so as to bring it within reasonable size and price.' The 116 black and white illustrations were completed about June 1876, again engraved by Cooper, and printed in 1876, although dated 1877. In spite of a reprint in 1877, *Bracebridge Hall* was not as popular as *Old Christmas*. Perhaps the most interesting aspect of this book was the binding, a uniform size, green colour, with gold embossed lettering identical to *Old Christmas*, but with the design of a young girl seated beneath a tree, a near copy of the designs of Caldecott's colleague and rival Kate Greenaway, who had published her first Calendars the year before.

With the success of these two books Caldecott's life began to alter. His frivolous days in the country changed to intense hours poring over the drawings for his next commission, while trying constantly to improve his style. He wrote to a Manchester friend:

I wish I had had a severe training for my present profession. Eating my dinners, so to speak. I have now got a workshop, and I sometimes wish that I was a workman. Art is long: life isn't.[35]

In another letter he described his dedication to his work.

I stick pretty close to business, pretty much in that admirable and attentive manner which was the delight, the pride, the exaltation of the great chiefs who strode it through the Manchester banking halls. Yes, I have not forsaken those gay—though perhaps to a heart yearning to be fetterless, irksome—scenes without finding that the world ever requires toil from those sons of labour who would be successful.[36]

His boyhood love of the country clouded his dedication and often filled him with guilt. Caldecott wrote to a friend from the country at Dodington, near Whitchurch, in the spring of 1875:

I feel I owe somebody an apology for staying in the country too long, but don't quite see to whom it is due, so I shall stay two or three days longer, and then I shall indeed hang my harp on a willow tree. It is difficult to screw up the proper amount of courage for leaving the lambkins, the piglets, the foals, the goslings, the calves, and the puppies.[37]

Caldecott moved from London to the French Riviera in January 1877 to ease his failing health. In the garden of the Hotel Splendid in Menton he and Armstrong spent long hours sketching and painting the scenery. His landscape served as studies for the backgrounds in over 300 sketches made from life. These were published in nearly sixty illustrations published in the *Graphic* (March to April 1877) accompanying a series of letters written by a fictitious English traveller, Corra, who described in words and sketches her experiences in Monte Carlo and Monaco. Henry Blackburn claimed that no such pictures of Monte Carlo and its neighbourhood had been sent home before; they were the ideal newspaper correspondent's letters. Indeed when Caldecott's work was compared with the feeble sketches by special correspondents of the *Illustrated London News* or *The Pictorial World* one can see how his deft, confident line and humorous chatty reporting endeared his work to thousands of potential English

'Chaffing the Milkmaid', illustration to *Bracebridge Hall* (1877)

'Rumpled Feathers', illustration to *Bracebridge Hall* (1877)

'The Apothecary', illustration to *Bracebridge Hall* (1877)

'The Farm House', illustration to *Bracebridge Hall* (1877)

'God Save the King', illustration to *Bracebridge Hall* (1877)

'Art is long, life is short'

the paper from its total reliance upon wood-engraved plates (even though Caldecott's work was engraved on wood and printed in sepia and colours by Edmund Evans). The paper's success led to Thomas founding *The Daily Graphic* twenty years later, London's first illustrated daily paper.

Caldecott's work appeared in nearly every summer and Christmas number of the *Graphic* from 1874 to after his death in 1886 (cf. appendix). His stories charmed and amused all who read them, for his intention was clear, as he explained to an admirer. 'Please say that my line is to make to smile the lunatic who has shown no sign of mirth for many months.'[38]

Caldecott's next important commission was another travelogue, *Breton Folk: An Artistic Tour in Brittany* by Henry Blackburn (1880) with 170 black and white illustrations engraved by J. D. Cooper. The book was the result of two summer tours in Brittany, with Blackburn. After the first summer an excerpt was published in *The Pictorial World* in 1874 (cf. appendix). In the preface Blackburn explains that the book was 'a series of sketches of a "black and white country" under its summer aspect; of a sombre land shrouded with white clouds, peopled with peasants in dark costumes, wide collars and caps, black and white cattle and magpies.' Caldecott's illustrations were made during his journey through miles of countryside, the artist stopping his trap to make brief sketches in notebooks of clouds, trees, animals or the local people. One grouping of women harvesting, 'Winnowing near St. Brieue', facing page 35 in the book, suggested a Millet painting, and it is interesting that Millet's *The Sower* was exhibited in 1873 at the Vienna Exhibition, where Caldecott was sent to make sketches for the New York *Daily Graphic.* Unfortunately Caldecott could not allow himself the full amount of time to record all he saw. He spent hours drawing the horse fair at Le Folgoet (which later provided material for a bas-relief exhibited at the Royal Academy in 1876) and interiors in village houses. These drawings were some of his clearest and most confident to date. He returned to London with greater assurance in his ability as a draughtsman which led to his next, and perhaps most important commission, the Picture Books.

Caldecott's early illustrations borrowed their style from the pen and ink sketches of John Leech and John Tenniel which appeared in periodicals and children's books. He was not alone in his admiration for these early masters—both George Du Maurier and Walter Crane acknowledged their debt to them. Soon Caldecott began to record the fleeting aspects of his surroundings in spontaneous, almost erratic, travel sketches. In time, however, his line loosened and the tight cross-hatched backgrounds, popular in illustrated Victorian novels, gave way to large expanses of white in which the figures appeared to dance in and out of the distance or along the margins, as in his work for the *Graphic*. When he was commissioned to illustrate the Picture Books he learned the need to define each illustration within a distinct outline, to colour it with expansive, even washes, all within the confines of a single frame or border. With the Picture Books it appeared at first that his early spontaneous style would have to be abandoned in favour of tightly-framed, full-page colour wood-engravings. Fortunately, the engraver Edmund Evans recognised Caldecott's unique ability to define the gesture of an animal with the flick of a pen and proposed using these brief sketches in

holiday makers. These and other *Graphic* works were, in fact, reissued in four separate volumes (cf. appendix).

Caldecott began his association with the *Graphic* about 1873. The paper had been founded in 1869 to take advantage of the opportunity of reporting the Franco-Prussian War of 1870, and eventually replaced the first important illustrated periodical, *Once a Week*, to become the most influential illustrated weekly in England, helping to revolutionise methods of English illustration. Gleeson White, the standard authority on English illustration, explained that the paper marked the close of the 'Sixties School' of wood-engraved illustration in favour of new methods, encouraged primarily by William Small and his followers. The first editor, William Luscon Thomas, attempted to draw attention to the social abuses in mid-Victorian England, the misery and poverty that existed alongside the greatest affluence, by reproducing such works as Fildes' *Application for Admission to a Casual Ward* and works of Hubert Herkomer, Frank Holl and Frederick Walker. Thomas wanted to reproduce the work of all artists regardless of their media, hoping to liberate

'Sketches at Trouville', introductory sketch for the series, published in the *Graphic,* October 1879

Caldecott made brief sketches for the series while staying at the Hotel de Paris, Trouville, where he wrote to William Clough, '....There are not many tip-top, right nobby, A-1, smashing swells here: but there are some nice-looking interesting folks' (Harvard letter 27 August 1879). He illustrated the pages with bathers and a self-portrait head bobbing in the distance under an umbrella.

'The Trap', illustration to *Breton Folk* (1880)

'The Ronde—a Country Dance', *Breton Folk* (1880)

This plate was later reproduced in *Artistic Travel* (1892) (cf. appendix).

combination with the finished full-page colour illustrations, and engraved them with the text, printed in brown ink.

Caldecott coloured his preliminary designs for the Picture Books in the subtlest pastel shades and relied upon brown outlines as opposed to the black used by his colleagues Walter Crane and Kate Greenaway. These colour illustrations, particularly those for *Come Lasses and Lads* and *The Farmer's Boy*, borrowed from eighteenth-century models. His women and children appear to have been copied from the portraits of Reynolds or Gainsborough, his horses hint of the works of Stubbs, and his idyllic landscapes suggest the watercolours of Cozens or Crome. Indeed, Caldecott's illustrations should be seen in relationship to those of his eighteenth-century forbears, for they mark a change from the satiric political caricatures of the Georgian era towards a more obvious humour enjoyed by both Victorian children and adults. Caldecott's predecessors included Hogarth, Gillray, Rowlandson, then, later, George Cruikshank and John Leech. The contemporary French critic and interpreter of English art for French periodicals, Ernest Chesneau, first established this analogy between Rowlandson, Gillray and Hogarth and the illustrators of *Punch*, the *Graphic* and, most importantly, the series of Routledge Picture Books illustrated by Caldecott, in his essay, 'Caricatures' from *The English School of Painting* (1885). He stated that Hogarth's desire was to present his subjects in suites, like theatrical acts of a comedy, which was, indeed, a technique utilised by Caldecott in his early comic sketches for local periodicals and the *Graphic*.

Caldecott shared Rowlandson's devotion to the scenes of humble eighteenth-century country life, where farmers attended fairs and markets with their livestock, and animals and men lived together on vast country estates or in small roadside cottages. In addition he borrowed Rowlandson's sure, swift line in his own attempt to revive the charms of Georgian England, as seen, for example, in his Picture Books *The Milkmaid*, *John Gilpin* and *Come Lasses and Lads*.

John Leech was employed as illustrator for *Punch* from 1841 to 1864 while Caldecott was still a child, but his mimicry of the manners and customs of his fellow countrymen set the mode for the young Caldecott and, indeed, for the works of his own contemporaries John Tenniel, George Du Maurier and Charles Keene.

Unfortunately, line drawing had declined in popularity during the 1870s. Henry Blackburn recognised the problem and made a plea for simpler use of line and for less elaborate illustrated books and periodicals in his Canto Lecture to the Royal Society of Arts in March 1875. He urged his colleagues to educate students in the use of pure line with pen and ink, a point also stressed by Walter Crane in lectures delivered at the Manchester School of Art, later published in *Line and Form*. 'Why is not drawing in line with pen and ink taught in more Government schools of art?' Blackburn asked. 'The readier method of pen and ink would be of great service, as a preparatory stage to wood drawing, but unfortunately drawing is taught in most cases as though the student intended to become a painter.'[39] Indeed, the American illustrator, Joseph Pennell observed in 1889 that England had so few line artists because the English artist tended to think of colour rather than line. The pen sketch was important only for speed in making a preparatory sketch for a painting.

Ironically, techniques of reproduction by wood-engravers depended upon the use of line by illustrators who employed one of two methods when drawing upon the wood block. The first, used by Caldecott and the artists of the 'Sixties School', involved a drawing made in pencil or pen and ink in simple outline to give a clear idea of the shapes and forms to be followed by the engraver. More lines could be added singly or in a series of cross-hatchings to suggest colour or tone, leaving blank those areas believed non-essential, which, when printed, appeared as white spaces 'for the imagination'. The engraver cut only the lines given by the illustrator, it being beyond his scope to add or leave out any of the artist's original lines.

The second technique used by line artists was credited to William Small, who used it to reproduce paintings of Luke Fildes, Hubert Herkomer and Lady Butler in several periodicals. His method originated the break from the 'Sixties School' of line towards reproduction of values or tones which, when carried further, led to reproductions by the photo-engraving or process method. The technique involved a painted finished picture on the block in black and white tonal washes which was left to the wood-engraver to interpret in lines. The artist's work and, indeed, his reputation was in the hands of the engraver, who added effects or subtracted areas according to his own preferences and skill.

The exact reproduction of an artist's work could not be left entirely in the hands of the engraver. For this reason and for the advantages of speed and exactitude the process of photo-engraving dealt a severe blow to the wood-engraving industry. Photography had in fact been used by the wood-engraver in transferring the original drawings to the boxwood block, using sensitive chemicals, but the process did not come into general use until the 1860s, when it was heralded as an important step towards raising the importance of pen and ink drawings as works of art. After photographic reproduction the original drawings would remain intact rather than be cut apart on a wood block. The new method was also important for reproducing the tones of a painting but, unfortunately, failed to provide as sharp a line as that achieved by the wood-engraver.

Caldecott was among the many young artists who attempted to draw for process reproduction; he worked for about a year on various methods including the Dawson Typographic Etching Process, which involved drawing upon a thin paraffin film. In addition, Dallastypes, using swelled gelatine for making photographic blocks, were made from Caldecott's works by Duncan C. Dallas who perfected the technique in 1875.[40] By 1877, however, Caldecott abandoned the process method in favour of the wood-engraver, for reasons Henry Blackburn explained.

He drew with greater freedom, as he expressed it, preferring, as so many illustrators do, to put in tints with a brush, to be rendered in line by skilful engravers. But at the same time he delighted in showing the power of line in drawing, studying 'the art of leaving out as a science', doing nothing hastily but thinking long and seriously before putting pen to paper, remembering as he always said, 'the fewer the lines, the less error committed.'[41]

Methods of process reproduction also helped raise the status of pen and ink illustrators to that of true artists capable of exhibiting their works as proper works of art. The most important early gallery for the 'black and white' artist was undoubtedly the Dudley Gallery, founded in 1864 by a group of amateur water colourists dissatisfied with the facilities for exhibiting work in London. Their

Illustration to *The Three Jovial Huntsmen* (1880)

gallery at the Egyptian Hall, Piccadilly, quickly became a popular exhibition centre. Many celebrated artists received early recognition at the Dudley Gallery, and, in addition to Caldecott, such painters and illustrators as Briton Riviere, Lady Butler, Whistler and Kate Greenaway exhibited their works there. A unique feature of the gallery was the 'Black and White' exhibition, held yearly from 1872 to 1875 between the closing of the annual watercolour exhibition and the opening of the cabinet oil paintings show. Pictures exhibited could be of any medium, except photography or architectural drawings, and works were selected by a committee of twelve which included Caldecott's friend George Du Maurier, Robert Macbeth, H. Stacy Marks, his old instructor at the Slade School, E. J. Poynter, William Small and Lumb Stocks.[42] Among the works exhibited at the first exhibition in 1872 were Whistler's etchings, about one hundred drawings on wood blocks and paper for the *Illustrated London News* and *Graphic*, described by an observer as being so brilliantly executed that they 'quite took one's breath away', and Caldecott's frame of four sepia ink drawings, 'Park Studies' (cf. appendix). Caldecott exhibited at the Dudley Gallery again at the third 'Black and White' exhibition in 1875.

Early in 1878 Caldecott began his fruitful business relationship with the famous colour printer and wood-engraver, Edmund Evans (1826-1905). In his reminiscences, Evans recorded his meeting with Caldecott at the artist's lodgings in Great Russell Street to propose illustrating a series of shilling toy books.[43] Caldecott agreed to produce about two books per year, an arrangement beginning in the autumn of 1878, when Evans engraved and printed the first two of an eventual sixteen Picture Books, *The House that Jack Built* and *John Gilpin*.

Edmund Evans' successful career as an engraver began with his early apprenticeship to Ebenezer Landells, the originator of *Punch*. During this time he worked with artists such as Birket Foster, T. Armstrong, the Dalziel brothers and Kate Greenaway's father, John Greenaway, then assistant to Landells. Evans formed his own wood-engraving business in 1847, and his first important work in colour was an edition of *The Poems of Oliver Goldsmith* (1858) with illustrations by Birket Foster. From 1865 he initiated a series of six-penny toy books, published partly by George Routledge and partly by Ward Lock, which established Evans as the foremost colour printer and most famous printer of children's books of the late Victorian period.[44] Evans may have employed as many as thirty assistants at his London offices at 4 Racquet Court, Fleet Street, where he maintained a constant control over all

Facsimile of letter

work produced, including directing the engravers as to the placement of lines on wood blocks, determining the tones and the mixture of coloured inks.[45] His skill at producing the original works of his artists was instrumental in the extraordinary success of three of his best known illustrators: Walter Crane, whose first work was engraved in the 1860s, Kate Greenaway, whose first successful book was engraved in 1878, and Caldecott himself. Evans described the process involved in printing:

The popular artists of the day were asked to supply drawings which were engraved on wood; then two 'transfers' from the engraved block, i.e. impressions while wet laid face down on plain blocks, then through the press so that the wet impression was 'set off' on the plain blocks, and used, one for a *Red* printing, the other for a Blue printing, the Red being engraved in graduation to get the lighter tints such as faces, hands, etc.—the Blue block being engraved to get the best result of texture, patterns or sky, crossing the blue over the red to get good effects of light and shade.... There were generally only three printings used—black, blue and red, or black, green and red; the very most was made of each block by engraving so as to get the best result for the money![46]

Although Evans normally used only three coloured blocks for his Picture Books, his earlier projects utilised from six to sixteen different blocks, painstakingly matched, or 'keyed', to produce graduated tones, closely resembling hand-coloured or coloured chromolithographed plates. He printed the first colour plates in the *Graphic* in 1872, a double page of the Albert Memorial, printed in colours and gold, and later engraved and printed Caldecott's masterful sketches for the same periodical (cf. appendix).

Unlike Kate Greenaway and Walter Crane, both of whom started work for Evans as little known artists, Caldecott began his association with the printer at the age of thirty-two, with an established reputation as the accomplished illustrator of *Old Christmas* and *Bracebridge Hall*. Indeed it was the success of these volumes which prompted Evans to offer Caldecott the Picture Book commissions, although they had worked together as early as 1873, when Caldecott illustrated six plates to *Frank Mildmay* (cf. appendix).

Their business relationship was founded upon a mutual trust. Unlike Kate Greenaway, who demanded the return of her drawings after reproduction, charging Evans only for their use while he bore the risk of small sales, Caldecott wanted a share in the speculative nature of his first Picture Books. He agreed to make the drawings and, if the books were sold, he would then be paid a fee. If they failed to sell, he would receive nothing. Evans explained the venture.

. . . . so I agreed to run all the risk of engraving the key blocks which he drew on wood; after he had coloured a proof I would furnish him, on drawing paper, I would engrave the blocks to be printed in as few colours as necessary. This was settled, the key block in *dark brown*, then a *flesh tint* for the faces, hands, and wherever it would bring the other colours as nearly as possible to his painted copy, a *red*, a *blue*, a *yellow*, and a *grey* (I was to supply paper and print 10,000 copies, which George Routledge & Sons have published for me).[47]

The Picture Books, with their coloured, wood-engraved illustrations, were Caldecott's major contribution to English illustration and, as such, are discussed individually in the captions to the plates. Sixteen Picture Books were published over a period of eight years with the following titles: *The House that Jack Built, John Gilpin* (1878); *Elegy on the Death of a Mad Dog* by Oliver Goldsmith, *The Babes in the Wood* (1879); *Sing a Song for Sixpence, Three Jovial Huntsmen,* (1880); *The Farmer's Boy, The Queen of Hearts* (1881); *The Milkmaid, Hey Diddle Diddle* and *Bye, Baby Bunting* (1882); *A Frog he would a-wooing go, The Fox Jumps over the Parson's Gate* (1883); *Come Lasses and Lads, Ride a Cock Horse to Banbury Cross* and *A Farmer went Trotting upon his Grey Mare* (1884); *An Elegy on the Glory of her Sex, Mrs. Mary Blaize* by Oliver Goldsmith, and *The Great Panjandrum Himself* (1885) (cf. appendix for reprinted editions and compilation volumes).

The first 10,000 copies sold out before another printing could be ordered, and the Picture Books became so popular that they were reissued later in separate volumes of four, eight, and sixteen titles bound together (cf. appendix). In a letter from Cannes (December 1878) Caldecott described the success of his first Picture Books.

Two or three notices have been read by the visitors to this hotel, and I am asked if I am any relation to the gifted artist. 30,000 [a figure conflicting with Evans'] of each book delivered to Christmas, more expected to sell straight away. Hope so. I get a small royalty—a small, small royalty.[48]

Caldecott's designs for the Picture Book series were unique. Unlike Walter Crane's designs which relied heavily upon ornate decoration and classically inspired figures, Caldecott's designs were based upon his supreme control of line; of the twenty-eight illustrations in *John Gilpin*,

Illustration to *The Great Panjandrum Himself* (1885)

Illustration to *Lob Lie-by-the-Fire* (1885)

only six were full-page colour plates, while the remainder were brief sketched vignettes scattered throughout the text. Both text and vignettes were printed in brown ink. Evans recounted Caldecott's working methods.

Shilling Toy Books, at that time, generally had blank pages at the back of the pictures: I proposed to have no blanks at all in these books: these slight illustrations were little more than outlines, but they were so racy and spontaneous, R.C. generally drew them from his friend where a man was wanted: his cats, dogs, showed how thoroughly he understood the anatomy of them. If the sketches came all right—he let them pass—if he was not satisfied with the results, he generally tore them up and burned them. They were made in pen and ink on smooth-faced writing paper, post 8vo. size, photographed on wood, and carefully engraved in 'fascimile'—Process work was not sufficiently perfected at this time to reproduce the drawings by this method.[49]

Caldecott spoke of his working methods in an interview with a journalist.

When Mr. Caldecott is contemplating one of his children's picture-books he chooses his own subjects, and after a good deal of serious consideration as to the method of treatment to be applied, he makes a blank book of the required size, and rapidly draws a number of sketches in the rough page for page as they will appear. This he uses as a guide when doing the actual work. Many of these finished sketches are done with a pen and brown ink on ordinary sheets of smooth white paper.[50]

Thirty such preliminary sketches for *The House that Jack Built* were published posthumously, as were the unfinished drawings for *Jack and the Beanstalk* (1886) (cf. appendix). Caldecott was keenly aware of the difficulties of engraving his delicate sketches and drawings. In a letter to Edmund Evans dated 5 March 1884, he described his impressions of Evans' work for his Picture Books.

I cannot understand—as I have told you—how those eyes in the key blocks of 2 or 3 of the pages in Picture Books came so dimly—and the lines in one girl's dress in p. 3 of *Come Lasses* came not at all. This is, I suppose—or rather, faintly conjecture, the result of trying to keep the lines & dots light in the engraving—altho. the girl in last (sic) coloured page but one of *Come Lasses* was meant to have dark eyes. I have thought the rendering of the faces this year better than ever before in the engraving—also the reproduction of the spirit of the touch all thro'—in fact. I think the engraving was a little over done in delicacy & some lines might have come out stronger than they have done. One or 2 artists who saw early proofs were well pleased.[51]

In the same letter to Evans, however, Caldecott expressed his desire to stop drawing for Picture Books.

I do not want to do any more of this kind: but I shall be glad to hear if you & Routledge have a strong opinion that a couple more should be done.... I wish to turn my attention to something else. I have an idea of another single book at 2/6 or so which might be successful. Books of several shillings seem to have difficulty in finding many customers in England. America is the place to publish more expensive books in.[52]

He did in fact illustrate two more Picture Books after 1884, in addition to a rather unsuccessful volume written by his brother, *Some of Aesop's Fables with Modern Instances*, by Rev. Alfred Caldecott with illustrations engraved by J. D. Cooper. Work on the book began in 1874, but it was not published until spring 1883. The 'modern instances' in the illustrations, suggested by Cooper, proved too dated, and the project was not popular. Caldecott wrote to a friend, 'Do not expect much from this book. When I see proofs of it I wonder and regret that I did not approach the subject more seriously'.[53] He also illustrated three books for the noted children's writer Juliana Horatio Ewing, the originator, in 1886, with her sister, Mrs. H. K. F. Gatty, of *Aunt Judy's Magazine*, for which Caldecott redesigned the cover. Caldecott had met Mrs. Ewing in London in June 1879 and agreed to illustrate the story of *Jackanapes* for the magazine, reissued in book form in 1884. He also illustrated Mrs. Ewing's *Daddy Darwin's Dovecote* (1884) and *Lob Lie-by-the-Fire* (1885). Most of his illustrations to Mrs. Ewing's works failed to maintain the high standards set by Caldecott in the Picture Books. As Gleeson White noted, 'Neither in the drawings nor in their engraving do you find anything which is above the average of its class'.[54]

In addition to a successful career as an illustrator, Caldecott attempted throughout his life to paint finished oils and watercolours and sculpt reliefs and statuettes suitable for exhibition at the Royal Academy, the Royal Manchester Institute, the Dudley Gallery, the Institute of

'St. Valentine's Day—The Ladies Battle', one of a pair of designs for a bas-relief, from *Randolph Caldecott Sketches* (1889)

Painters in Water Colour and the Grosvenor Gallery (cf. appendix). The Caldecott estate sale catalogue listed forty-one 'finished pictures and studies in oil' and twelve different sculptures in wax, plaster and bronze, a collection which did not include several known terra-cotta statuettes completed after his visit to Brittany in 1874.

With the encouragement of his friends, Caldecott had begun painting in oil and watercolour while living in Manchester, where he exhibited his first painting in 1869. In London Thomas Armstrong had encouraged him to draw and paint the birds which formed the basis for decorative panel paintings used in room interiors and for painted furniture. Birds were, in fact, to become his most favourite subject, and he diligently studied them from life and as mounted specimens in museum collections. These drawings served as studies for illustrations to books such as *Daddy Darwin's Dovecote*, *The Owls of Olynn Belfry* and *What the Blackbird Saw*. One can imagine the young Caldecott pouring over exhibitions of birds without regard for time when he recorded in his diary that Christmas Eve 1874 was 'spent in the caverns of the British Museum, making a drawing, and measuring a skeleton of a white stork' or that on 30 December 1874 he was 'at British Museum; had storks out of cases to examine insertion of wing feathers.'[55] Presumably these studies were for painting on wood for a wardrobe. When he exhibited his first painting, *There were Three Ravens Sat on a Tree*, at the Royal Academy in 1876 (page 49), members of the Academy strongly urged him to devote all his energies to painting. Unfortunately, his book illustrations demanded most of his time, and he had to relegate only spare moments to painting in oil. While staying on the Riviera in 1876, however, he managed to paint several landscapes in oil and water colour which served as studies for backgrounds later drawn and engraved for the *Graphic*. These landscapes suffered from poor reproduction, and Caldecott wrote to a prospective patron in response to a landscape commission that 'The drawings that G. so kindly enquires about are not in my line. I would rather not attempt to paint what I imagine he wants—proper professional water colour landscape painter's work. . . . not but what I would if I could!'[56] He did, however, succeed in producing a considerable number of paintings, and a journalist remarked in 1884 that 'Last year, besides his ordinary work, he was able to complete six water-colours and one or two canvases of considerable size'.[57]

Indeed, Caldecott felt the need, while engaged on sketchy drawings for humorous children's books, to practise the more concentrated aspects of painting which required serious study.

Caldecott began sculpting as a child, cutting animals from blocks of wood and moulding in clay. As previously mentioned, while in London he served under Jules Dalou, the French sculptor, and accepted Thomas Armstrong's help and advice on modelling in wax for bas-reliefs. His first terra-cotta statuettes were based upon his experiences as 'special reporter', a terra-cotta of the Tichborne trial, for instance, appearing in 1874. Later in the same year Caldecott completed his first bas-relief hunting scene. His visit to Brittany in 1874 provided material for a group of terra-cotta statuettes, including 'At Guingamp, Brittany' (1874), which Caldecott regarded as only 'a rough sketch', a 'recollection in clay'. The modelling for these efforts was undoubtedly crude, but they served as technical studies for several more important bas-reliefs, such as 'A Horse Fair in Brittany', which was exhibited at the Royal Academy in 1876 and hailed by a critic of the *Saturday Review* (10 June 1876).

Of low relief—taking the Elgin frieze as a standard—one of the purest we have seen for many a day is Mr. Caldecott's bas-relief, 'A Horse Fair in Brittany'. Here a simple and almost rude incident in nature has been brought within the laws and symmetry of art.'

Caldecott was also commissioned to sculpt work for decorative room interiors and chimney pieces—for instance, in 1879, the architect George Aitchison, who owned a cast of his first hunting relief, engaged him to design the capitals for columns in Frederick Leighton's Arab Hall, above which stretched a gold mosaic frieze designed by Caldecott's friend and competitor Walter Crane.

As a draughtsman Caldecott experimented with various graphic printing techniques, and his diary entry for 25 January 1875 includes a reference to 'a dry point sketch of a Quimperle Brittany woman'. The Victoria and Albert Museum, London, owns an early lithograph of a young boy with horses standing against a wall (E 3696-1927), while the Brasenose Club exhibition catalogue listed the etching 'The Sportsman's Return', owned by Thomas Armstrong. In a letter to Edmund Evans dated 5 March 1884 he proposed a series of prints suitable for framing.

....that something even higher than we have done together might be tried. Something to frame. Decorative things sell for framing. I have talked of a set of hunting scenes—you know. Perhaps we may try one, or a picture of a separate subject and see how the public or the Fine Art Society will receive it.[58]

Unfortunately this venture never materialised, although there is evidence of a series of coloured glass transparencies after Caldecott's designs for the Picture Books, possibly produced by Frederick Warne. A collection of twelve is in the Manchester Reference Library.

Caldecott also experimented with chalk on brown paper as a rapid medium to record his large decorative designs and for use in caricatures. His estate sale catalogue listed seven chalk drawings, one diary entry (8 July 1872) notes that he was 'engaged on chalk caricatures all day'.[59] It is interesting to observe his talents for caricature turned toward one of the masters of the craft when he executed a series of pencil caricatures of 'Ape', Carlo Pelligrini, whose works for *Vanity Fair* remain classics of the genre.[60]

Caldecott moved in the autumn of 1879 to a small country house, Wybournes, Kemsing, near Sevenoaks, Kent, where he spent many days drawing in the countryside he loved so much. He married Marion Brind in March 1880, the same year he was elected member of the Manchester Academy of Fine Arts, and they honeymooned in Menton, returning to a life divided between London and Kemsing. During the early 1880s Caldecott was occupied with commissions for *Punch* and *Graphic*, and with illustrating the books of Mrs. Ewing and a selection of *Fables de la Fontaine* (1885). He also completed the twelfth Picture Book and designed small vignette illustrations to the works of his friend the Lancashire poet Edwin Waugh (cf. appendix). The variety of work at this time led to his travelling to numerous parts of the Continent and throughout England: in May 1881 he visited Menton again, returning to England in the autumn. From December 1881 to April 1882 he spent time in Florence, occupying the rooms of the Brazilian vice consulate, and in 1882 he left Kemsing and took a 21 year lease on Broomfield, a country house in Frensham, Farnham, Surrey, where he lived until 1885. He also purchased in the same year a small house in Kensington, at 24 Holland Street, where he built a small studio in the garden, so that the last period of his life was spent commuting between London and Farnham. He customarily sketched the Surrey countryside into his Picture Book illustrations, journeying to London only when a model was necessary. While in the country Caldecott maintained a rigorous schedule, rising at eight o'clock, working from ten to noon, then walking, riding and hunting twice a week, as well as managing his small farm from which he derived a modest income and great satisfaction.

Caldecott sold his house in England and sailed for America in October 1885, on the advice of Frederick Locker, his intimate friend, with the hopes that the warmer climate in Florida would ease his rapidly worsening health. During the journey he recorded aspects of American life in 'American Facts and Fancies, I and II' (cf. appendix), a commission for the *Graphic*. Caldecott arrived in New York, and planned to travel down the eastern coast, through the South and across the continent to California, returning over the mountains. The initial journey was rough, and Caldecott contracted acute gastritis in Florida, during that state's worse cold spell in fifty years. Before his devoted friend Armstrong could join him to try and revive the artist, Caldecott died on 13 February 1886, aged forty, his career as an artist spanning a mere ten years.

It is ironic that the very country which had given Caldecott his first commissions in *The Daily Graphic* and helped promote his successful career had now taken away his chances to further that career. However, his work is still revered in America and receives a fitting contemporary tribute in the annual awarding of the Caldecott Medal to the artist who has illustrated the 'most distinguished American picture book for children in the United States during the preceeding year', a selection made by the Children's Service Division of the American Library Association.

Caldecott's amiable, often humorous nature was founded upon his regard for his many friends who, after his death, formed a committee to place a memorial in St. Paul's Cathedral, near that of Cruikshank. His letters to them are filled with delightful sketches, revealing a man of great sensitivity, with a highly developed sense of humour

and an ability to record an impression in a moment's time. His life-long friend William Clough offered the following tribute.

If the art, tender and true as it is, be not of the highest, yet the artist is expressed in his work as perhaps few others have been. Nothing to be regretted—all of the clearest — an open-air pure life—a clean soul. Wholesome as the England he loved so well. Manly, tolerant, and patient under suffering. None of the friends he made did he let go. No envy, malice, or uncharitableness spoiled him; no social flattery or fashionable success, made him forget those he had known in his early years.[61]

Once when asked to make portrait drawings of a number of his contemporaries for an album, he refused for fear 'some touch of caricature or keen insight should hurt any one of them.'[62]

Indeed even the formidable president of the Royal Academy, Sir Frederick Leighton, addressed the Academy on 1 May 1886.

.... such, I think, was an artist whose name I am compelled to pronounce to-night—withal an artist whose works are in every English hand, and are cherished in every English home; whose sweet and dainty grace has not been, in its kind, surpassed; whose humour was as quaint as it was inexhaustible, and his mirth bubbling and contagious; a pure and wholesome artist in whom each of us has lost a friend; for who amongst us, gentlemen, is not in some degree poorer by the death of Randolph Caldecott?

Extravagant claims that his reputation had spread faster than that of any artist who had ever lived were made following his death, and it is true that his influence had spread to France. A French edition of his English periodical illustrations was published in 1882 and he exhibited works at the Paris Salon in 1881, so it is not surprising that Gauguin as well as Van Gogh acknowledged their admiration for his work.

Van Gogh praised Caldecott's early illustrations when writing to his brother.

Recently I saw a new edition of R. Caldecott's picture books and bought two of them, namely, illustrations of Washington Irving's Sketch Book, which both together cost a shilling now. There is a description of Christmas in a little village, at the beginning of this century. Those small drawings are pithy, like Jacque's, for instance, or Menzel's. When you come, you must look at the wood engravings again. Right now there are some people like Caldecott, for instance, who are quite original and highly interesting.[63]

When Gauguin met the English painter A. S. Hartrick at Pont Aven, in about 1886, he mentioned his admiration for Caldecott's drawings of geese, presumably from *John Gilpin* (1878), which he praised highly, exclaiming, 'That was the true spirit of drawing'.[64]

English artists were equally captivated by Caldecott's work. Kate Greenaway lamented her own lack of imagination when she saw Caldecott's designs for *Hey Diddle Diddle* (1882). Caldecott was in fact on several occasions mistakenly identified as Kate Greenaway's husband. He was not intrigued by the possibility and wrote to a friend in 1880, 'She is, as you ask me, nearly thirty—maybe more—and not beautiful.'[65] Perhaps Miss Greenaway felt Edmund Evans was going too far when he suggested a joint commission shared between the two artists, for Mavor's *English Spelling Book* (1885). Caldecott made a preliminary drawing for the book, but Miss Greenaway flatly refused to be part of the venture and accepted the commission alone.[66]

Walter Crane also recognised Caldecott's talent and had

assisted the artist when he first arrived in London, giving him advice on publishers to approach. They became good friends as Caldecott explained in a letter to William Clough dated 8 July 1883, with Crane's autograph enclosed.

He is a dearer (sic) man; but he does not enough follow his natural bent. He is in the thrall of the influence of the early and most intellectual Italian painters and draughtsmen.[67]

Crane also recorded his respect for Caldecott's work in his treatise *Of the Decorative Illustration of Books Old and New* (1896).

The young Beatrix Potter knew and admired Caldecott's work as well. Her father had purchased two small pen and ink sketches to *A Frog he would a-wooing go* and the set of sketches to *The Three Jovial Huntsmen* which must certainly have influenced her own drawings for children's books.[68]

Caldecott's influence was carried into the twentieth century by two artist-illustrators, Hugh Thomson (1860-1920) and the American-born Edwin Austin Abbey (1852-1911) and through the interpretive writing of Austin Dobson (1840-1921).

Hugh Thomson was the first of the Cranford School of illustrators, those artists who abandoned the 'nineties style of Beardsley for the delicacy of an eighteenth-century mode. Thomson had served as apprentice to Marcus Ward, the Belfast publisher of works by Kate Greenaway and Walter Crane, and had moved to London as staff artist for the recently-founded *English Illustrated Magazine* when he met Caldecott, who had illustrated articles for the periodical (cf. appendix). Caldecott's work clearly made an impact upon Thomson's style, and the link between the two men grew even stronger when Macmillan asked Thomson to illustrate the new volumes in their posthumous revival of Caldecott's Washington Irving series. Thomson illustrated volumes 5 and 6 in addition to Goldsmith's *Vicar of Wakefield* (1890) and Mrs. Gaskell's *Cranford* (1891). These were published and bound in the same green covers with gold embossed design as the earlier Caldecott volumes, but while Thomson's illustrations relied heavily upon Caldecott's translation of the past, they lacked the delicate spontaneity of the master's line and proper understanding of the placement of illustrations within the body text. Thomson was, nevertheless, quite popular and even shared a joint exhibition (1891) of works at the Fine Art Society with no one less than Kate Greenaway.

Edwin Austin Abbey's acquaintance with Caldecott's work came during the years 1871 to 1874 when he was a 'special artist reporter' for *Harper's Magazine*, which published Caldecott's *Harz Mountains* in excerpt form in 1873 (cf. appendix). Abbey illustrated the *Harper's* serial 'Our London Scrapbook' with small engravings strikingly similar in style to Caldecott's early work for *London Society* and in 1883 moved to London, where he became a friend of such notable figures as Whistler, Alma-Tadema, Fildes, and Caldecott, to whom he was especially close. Abbey and Caldecott were elected members of the Savile Club, often dined together in London and, when Caldecott left for America in 1885, Abbey wrote to his friend Charles Parsons in New York and to a cousin in Florida asking them to look after the then ailing artist. Abbey's illustrations to editions of eighteenth-century literature—Sheridan's *Comedies* (1885), *Selections from the Poetry of Robert Herrick* (1882) and Pope's *Ode to*

'Somebody's Coming!', published in *The Pictorial World,* May 1874

Sketch, published in *Pall Mall Gazette*

Solitude (1890) with a preface by Austin Dobson—again drew upon Caldecott's recreations of the Georgian era.

The poet Henry Austin Dobson played an important role in the revival of interest in eighteenth-century literature and art. In addition to writing biographies of Hogarth (1879) and Goldsmith (1888), Dobson also interpreted Caldecott's work in the introduction to *The Complete Collection of Randolph Caldecott's Pictures and Songs* (1887). A fervent admirer of Caldecott's work, he wrote to the artist in 1881 asking for a drawing 'in the Bracebridge Hall manner' for a projected illustrated edition of Goldsmith's 'Beau Tibbs' from *The Citizen of the World* (Tibbs was a favourite character of Caldecott's). Caldecott also illustrated Dobson's edition of the *Vicar of Wakefield* (1883), and his poem, 'Vauxhall', from the *Magazine of Art*.

Randolph Caldecott's major importance to the history of English illustration was his ability to record the subtleties of late Victorian life, often masked in the Georgian guise, all with the flick of a pen or brush. His keen eye and spontaneous manner made his work unique even by present-day standards, and Joseph Pennell claimed in 1889 that 'There is no one in England who has ever equalled him in this respect, and I very much doubt if any one anywhere ever surpassed him'.[69] His short life was surprisingly prolific, and he will always be remembered for bringing the rare element of individuality, so masterfully preserved in the wood engraving and colour printing of Edmund Evans, into the periodicals and children's books of the 1870s and 1880s, and into his attempts at painting and sculpting. Although his illustrations are often linked with those of his colleagues Walter Crane and Kate Greenaway, his work was even more individual, for he avoided falling prey to public taste, either to the Aesthetic Movement's coyness or the exoticism and overintellectualisation of the Pre-Raphaelites. Crane's overdecorated and rather staid academic figures contrast to Caldecott's dancing farmers or scurrying dogs, while Kate Greenaway's simperingly repetitive children were surpassed by his cherubic boys and girls bouncing atop galloping ponies and racing down old dusty roads. Even more importantly Caldecott could draw animals with an easy accuracy which put Kate Greenaway's rat-like cats or Walter Crane's goat-like poodles to shame. A study of his illustrations shows a continual development, an opening up, a freeness spawned from endless hours of recording nature, travelling with inch-square sketchbooks pulled from his waistcoat pocket to capture the line of a face or the wag of a tail. As Austin Dobson wrote, Caldecott could capture in line the England one longed to experience.

The open-air life of England, with all its freshness and breeziness, its pastoral seduction and its picturesque environment, is everywhere present in his work. He has the art, too, of being elegant without being effeminate, and of being tender without being mawkish.... No taint clings to them of morbid affection or sickly sentiment: they are the general pictorial utterances of a manly, happy nature delighting in innocent pleasure, and dowered as few English artists have been with gifts of refinement and grace.[70]

Caldecott's illustrations were essential elements of a short-lived though prolific artistic career, as summarised in a memorial poem by 'H.E.D.' in the *Graphic*.

Alas poor Caldecott! we hoped in vain
We should not lose thy presence yet awhile.
Thou hadst no rival in thine own quaint style;
Vacant thy place may evermore remain.
Thy pencil drew, with loving, faithful care,
Each phase of human nature in its turn.
So that one looked and laughed, but yet could learn
To love all men the more for what was there.
Old folks would smile, and seem to see once more
The men and manners of a day gone by,
Whilst infants o'er thy 'Picture Books' would pore,
And feast on Dreamland scenes with wondering eye.[71]

Diagram, 'A Mad Dog'

[1] *The Complete Collection of Randolph Caldecott's Contributions to the Graphic,* 1888, p. 1. Caldecott's school master James Harris used to show a sketch in an old Virgil by his young pupil, of Aeneas carrying off his father Anchises from the ruins of Troy, cf. *Manchester Quarterly,* July 1886.

[2] Obituary, *Manchester Quarterly,* July 1886.

[3] Letter in collection Williams and Glyn's Bank, Manchester; an article in the *Pall Mall Gazette,* 4 January 1884, by an unknown journalist explained that Caldecott 'was transferred to a bank in uncongenial Manchester'.

[4] Obituary, *Manchester Courier,* 16 February 1886.

[5] *The Sphinx,* Vol. III, 23 April 1870, p. 130.

[6] See commemorative volume, *Williams Deacon's 1771-1970,* Manchester, 1971, p. 121.

[7] Victoria and Albert Museum print room, E. 3656-3696-1927. The Williams and Glyn's Bank, Manchester, also own two early pen and ink sketches dated 1870.

[8] Harvard letter 18 August 1885.

[9] Alfred Derbyshire, *An Architect's Reminiscences,* 1897, p. 30.

[10] Ibid. p. 83.

[11] *The Sphinx, op.cit.,* p. 130. The club rules (1870) listed 200 ordinary members, 50 country, 20 associates and honorary members distinguished in art, science or literature with an entrance fee of £3 and 3 shillings.

[12] Advertisement, *The Sphinx,* Vol. II, 25 December 1869, p. 315.

[13] *Pall Mall Gazette, op.cit.*

[14] *Ibid.*

[15] Henry Blackburn, *Randolph Caldecott,* 1886, p. 13.

[16] *Ibid.,* p. 14.

[17] Gleeson White, *English Illustration: The 'Sixties' 1855-1870,* 1897, p. 55.

[18] Blackburn, *op.cit.,* pp. 16-17.

[19] *Ibid.,* p. 61.

[20] *Ibid.,* p. 20.

[21] *Pall Mall Gazette,* 7 January 1884.

[22] Blackburn, *op.cit.,* p. 32.

[23] *Pall Mall Gazette, op.cit.*

[24] Both letters in Parker collection, Harvard University Library.

[25] Blackburn, *op.cit.,* pp. 30, 52. Caldecott's step brother Rev. Alfred Caldecott wrote to Armstrong on his brother's death, 'The friendship of you stands out in my mind as one of the significant and real facts of human life. . . . You hardly know yourself, you cannot know, how really you were elder brother to him by a tie that makes me doubt the vaunted closeness of the bond of blood.' See L. M. Lamont, *Thomas Armstrong. A Memoir,* 1912, p. 60.

[26] *Ibid.,* pp. 34-9. Caldecott was also a member of the London Arts Club until he resigned. The letter of resignation is in the Victoria and Albert Museum Library.

[27] *Ibid.,* p. 35.

[28] Blackburn, *op.cit.,* p. 54.

[29] Harry Furniss, *The Confessions of a Caricaturist,* Vol. I, 1901, p. 68.

[30] Complete text of the lecture in *Journal of the Society of Arts,* 12 March 1875, p. 366ff.

[31] *The Pictorial World,* Vol. I, No. 1, 7 March 1874, p. 2. C. N. Williamson in his article, 'Illustrated Journalism in England', explained that *The Pictorial World* resembled the *Graphic* in size, shape and appearance but was inferior for its artists' works and engravings. See *Magazine of Art,* Vol. XIII, 1890, pp. 393-4.

[32] *The Pictorial World,* Vol. IV, No. 95, 25 December 1875, p. 275. The article included illustrations from the book.

[33] Blackburn, *op.cit.,* p. 105.

[34] Mary G. Davis, *Randolph Caldecott, An Appreciation,* 1946, p. 29.

[35] Blackburn, *op.cit.,* p. 97.

[36] *Ibid.,* p. 118.

[37] *Ibid.,* p. 127.

[38] *Ibid.,* pp. 152-3.

[39] Henry Blackburn, *The Art of Illustration,* 1894, p. x.

[40] For a complete description of the process see A. Brothers, *Photography, Its History, Processes, Apparatus and Materials,* 1899, plate 35.

[41] Blackburn, *op.cit.,* p. 126.

[42] H. S. Marks, *Pen & Pencil Sketches,* Vol. I, 1894, pp. 173-4.

[43] Ruari McLean, *Reminiscences of Edmund Evans,* 1967, p. 25.

[44] *Ibid.,* p. xvi.

[45] *Ibid.,* p. ix.

[46] *Ibid.,* pp. 26-7.

[47] *Ibid.,* p. 56.

[48] Harvard letter 13 December 1878.

[49] McLean, *op.cit.,* p. 56.

[50] *Pall Mall Gazette, op.cit.*

[51] Letter in Victoria and Albert Museum Library (RC K9).

[52] *Ibid.*

[53] Blackburn, *op.cit.,* p. 96.

[54] White, *op.cit.,* p. 86.

[55] Blackburn, *op.cit.,* pp. 87, 115.

[56] Blackburn, *op.cit.,* pp. 152-4.

[57] *Pall Mall Gazette, op.cit.*

[58] Letter in Victoria and Albert Museum Library (RC K9).

[59] Blackburn, *op.cit.,* p. 31.

[60] Lamont, *op.cit.,* p. 213.

[61] *Manchester Quarterly, op.cit.*

[62] Obituary, *Manchester City News,* 20 February 1886. Written by 'one of four', presumably one of Caldecott's closest friends.

[63] *Complete Letters of Vincent Van Gogh,* Vol. I, 1958, p. 544.

[64] A. S. Hartrick, *A Painter's Pilgrimage through Fifty Years,* 1938, p. 33.

[65] Davis, *op.cit.,* p. 34.

[66] Phillips sale catalogue No. 18.837, 1975, item no. 89.

[67] Harvard letter 8 July 1883.

[68] Leslie Linder, *The Journal of Beatrix Potter,* 1966, p. 64. These works were later presented by Beatrix Potter (Mrs. W. Heelis) to the City Art Gallery, Manchester.

[69] Joseph Pennell, *Pen Drawing and Pen Draughtsmanship,* 1889, p. 179.

[70] *The Complete Collection of Randolph Caldecott's Pictures and Songs,* 1887, p. ii.

[71] Preface, *The Complete Collection of Randolph Caldecott's Contributions to the 'Graphic',* 1888.

'Public distress, Sir, is all humbug', illustration to *Bracebridge Hall* (1877)

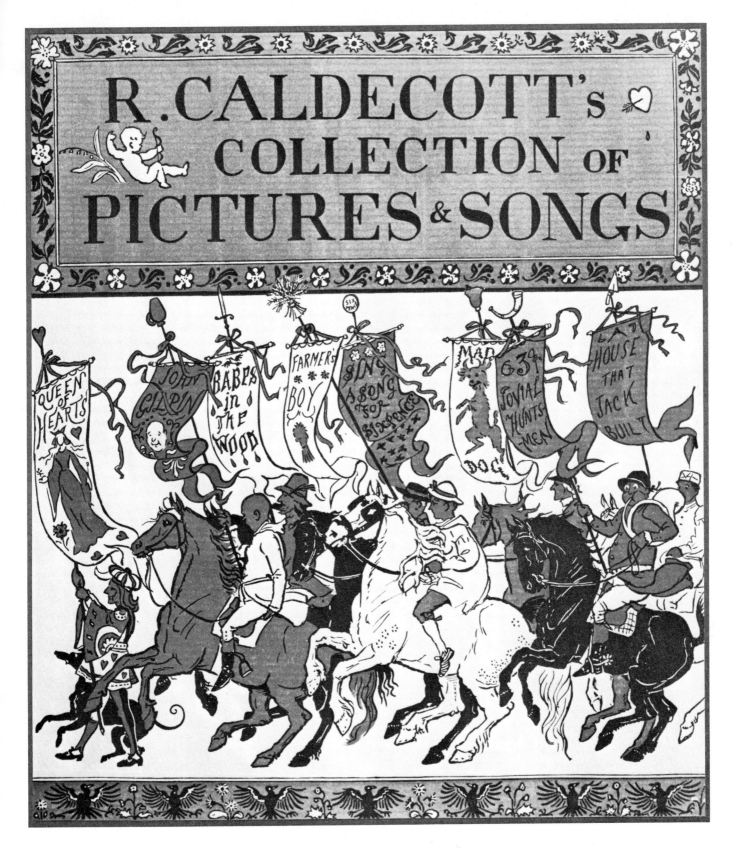

Cover illustration, *R. Caldecott's Collection of Pictures and Songs* (1883)

A new edition of the first eight Picture Books published in one volume, priced 10s 6d. Caldecott was concerned with the cost of his books after the first two were published, hoping they would reach a wider public. He wrote to Frederick Locker in 1880, 'As for myself my price is just the same on the last books as on the first. There has been no change, & I arranged the price with E. Evans after finding out how much could be afforded out of the sum that Routledges would pay for the books. I tried hard last winter to get R's to pay more. They say that the sellers won't pay more for them. I fear that the only way for me to get more is by raising the price of the books—putting them in stiffer cover apart from 1st & last pictures. Or should I threaten or stick out or something! Do you think ½ of the present sale would be found for a 2s book? . . . Evans wishes me to do 2 more in some terms to complete another volume of 4' (Harvard letter 24 November 1880).

Cover illustration, *R. Caldecott's Second Collection of Pictures and Songs* (1885)

This volume included the last eight Picture Books in one volume and was issued in the same year as *The Panjandrum Picture Book* and *The Hey Diddle Diddle Picture Book*.

Cover illustration, *The Panjandrum Picture Book* (1885)

The last four Picture Books were published together in a cloth-bound oblong format. The book was compiled from Caldecott's last important work for children, published at the time Kate Greenaway's career was reaching its height: her second, and most popular book, *Marigold Garden,* was published in the same year.

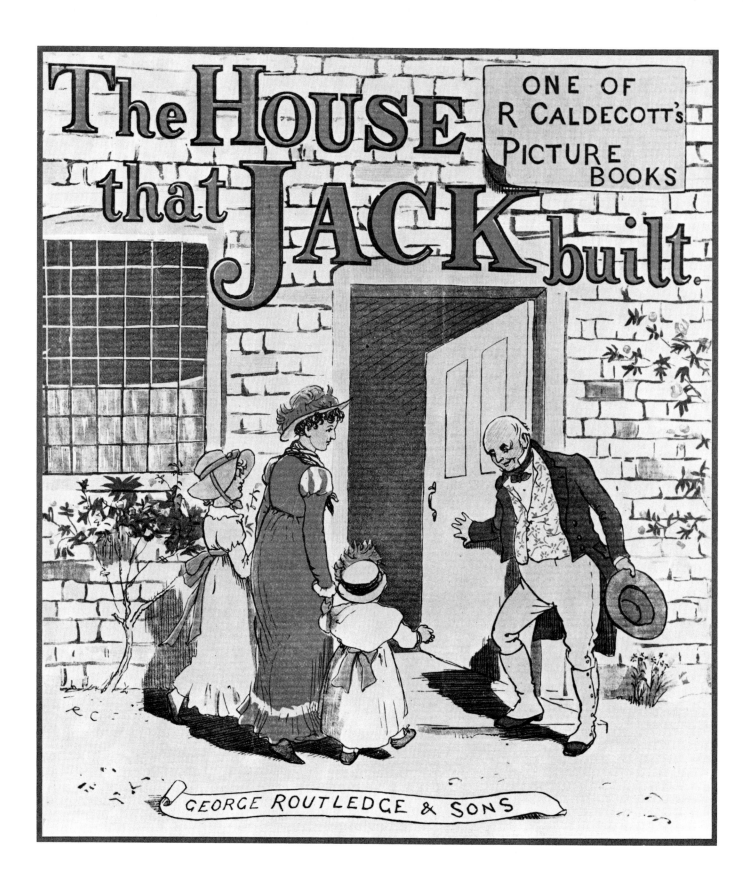

Cover illustration, *The House that Jack Built* (1878)

This was Caldecott's first commission for the Picture Book series. The books were priced at one shilling each, with a minimum of nine full-colour illustrations and twenty line drawings printed in brown. This book contained thirty-three colour illustrations engraved and printed by Edmund Evans. The popular rhyme was also published as one of Walter Crane's earliest children's books in 1865 for Ward, Lock & Tyler's New Shilling series and another version, with illustrations by E. Mordant Cox, was published in 1880.

'This is the House that Jack Built', *The House that Jack Built* (1878)

An amusing controversy arose over this illustration, which was explained in Caldecott's obituary (cf. *Manchester City News,* 20 February 1886). 'One of the notices in our local press errs in saying that *A House that Jack Built* contains a likeness of a late and highly esteemed banker. The artist denied that it was so and we must accept his denial.'

'This is the cat,
That killed the rat,
That ate the malt
That lay in the house that Jack built.'

The House that Jack Built (1878)

(above)
Crouching Cat (c. 1874)
London, Victoria and Albert Museum. Terra-cotta statuette

Caldecott modelled this cat about 1874 from studies made of a live cat, a dead carcass and a skeleton (cf. Blackburn, *Randolph Caldecott,* 1886, p. 114). The pose is duplicated in the cat illustration in *The House that Jack Built* (1878).

(right)
'Maiden & Man', *Lightning Sketches for 'The House that Jack Built'* (1899)

Although Caldecott's friend Thomas Armstrong forbade their publication, the thirty preliminary sketches for the Picture Book were finally engraved by Edmund Evans and published in brown ink, in aid of the London Hospital. Caldecott's widow believed any gesture to preserve the quality of her husband's work was important and felt that these sketches, if published alone, would be misinterpreted as slight examples unworthy of attention. She wanted a proper explanation as to their intent printed in the book's introduction, but the only text, written by A. Trevor-Battye, claimed '....these lightning sketches will come with a curious sense as ghosts—ghosts of the pictures known so well....see how Randolph Caldecott could spin it off!'

'This is the cock that crowed in the morn,
That waked the priest all shaven and shorn....'

The House that Jack Built (1878)

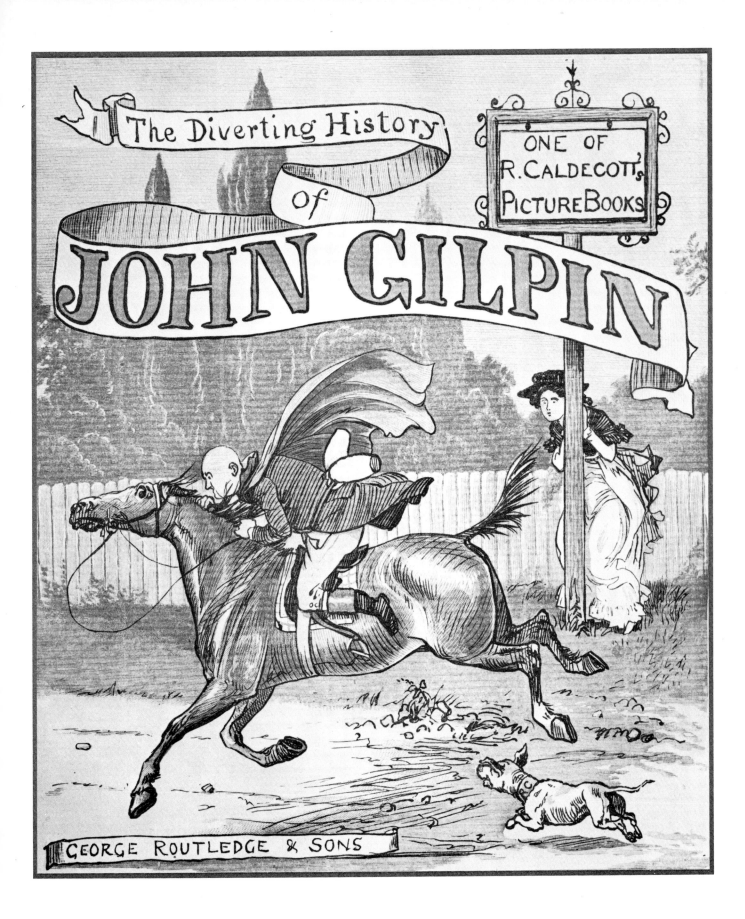

Cover illustration, *The Diverting History of John Gilpin* by William Cowper (1878)

The first of two annual Picture Books by Caldecott, this was unique for its two double-page colour illustrations. The first printing of 10,000 copies sold out before a second printing could be ordered, and in 1880 Caldecott wrote to Frederick Locker about the possibility of a German edition.

'At Edmonton his loving wife
From the balcony spied
Her tender husband, wondering much
To see how he did ride.

'Stop, stop, John Gilpin!—Here's the house!
They all at once did cry;
The dinner waits, and we are tired;
Said Gilpin—So am I.'

The Diverting History of John Gilpin (1878)

The ducks, geese and dogs in this and other plates in the book were praised by both Van Gogh and Gauguin for their life-like qualities (cf. Hartrick, *A Painter's Pilgrimage,* 1939, p. 33).

'The dogs did bark, the children screamed,
Up flew the windows all;
And every soul cried out, 'Well done!'
As loud as he could bawl.

'Away went Gilpin—who but he?
His fame soon spread around;
He carries weight! he rides a race!
'Tis for a thousand pound!'

The Diverting History of John Gilpin (1878)

The complete title of Cowper's story, first published in 1785, was 'The Diverting History of John Gilpin: Showing how he went farther than he intended, and came safe home again', and describes Gilpin's ride, with flasks of wine strapped to his belt for his family's dinner, through Cheapside, Islington, Edmonton, and reluctantly on to Ware.

Cover illustration, *Elegy on the Death of a Mad Dog* by Oliver Goldsmith (1879)

Caldecott's third Picture Book was originally printed with a pale pink card cover. The original drawing for the title page was owned by Frederick Locker, the poet of *London Lyrics* and Caldecott's life-long friend.

'The dog, to gain some private ends, went mad, and bit the man', *Elegy on the Death of a Mad Dog* (1879)

This story, written by Oliver Goldsmith and here 'sung by Master Bill Primrose', is set in Islington, where a notoriously good natured man adopts a dog which becomes jealous of his master's affection towards a cat and bites him. The dog is tracked down and found dead while the injured man miraculously recovers from the bite.

'The wound it seemed both sore and sad to every Christian eye', *Elegy on the Death of a Mad Dog* (1879)

Caldecott's vivid depiction of illness, here in the jaundiced yellow-grey face of the man, may be the result of his working on the book when he was '. . . . very very stomachily seedy at Florence & most were arranged & planned there. I scribbled out the plan of 1 book in the train between Florence & Bologna' (Harvard letter 8 November 1879).

Cover illustration, *The Babes in the Wood* (1879)

Unlike most of the Picture Books, the cover for *The Babes in the Wood* was printed on pale green card with an ominous black background. Another version of the story was published earlier as *Routledge's Large-size Sixpenny Toy Books No. 3,* with illustrations by E. H. Corbould, whose *Punch* illustrations were contemporary to Caldecott's work for the periodical.

(right)
John Gilpin's Ride
Manchester, Whitworth Art Gallery. Watercolour, bodycolour, pen and ink.

This highly finished painting depicting Gilpin riding past the Bell Inn, Edmonton, was probably painted after the Picture Book illustrations, although there is a similarity to the figure pose of Gilpin in the frontispiece. The original drawings to the Picture Book are owned by the Victoria and Albert Museum, London and Birmingham City Art Gallery.

SORE SICKE THEY WERE
AND LIKE TO DYE

'Sore sicke they were and like to dye', *The Babes in the Wood* (1879)

The story relates the plight of two children whose dying parents give them into the care of an uncle. He sells them to two ruffians who take them into the forest to be killed. The children ride off in an illustration reminiscent of *Ride a Cock Horse to Banbury Cross* (1884), while 'Rejoicing with a merry minde, They should on cock-horse ride.'

(left)
'The Mad Dog', *Elegy on the Death of a Mad Dog* by Oliver Goldsmith (1879)

The subtlety of Evans' colour printing from Caldecott's drawings, especially the dog's glazed stare, and Caldecott's skill in drawing animals, combined to make this Landseer-like plate unique to Caldecott's *oeuvre*.

'Death of the children', *The Babes in the Wood* (1879)

The children wander aimlessly, eventually die and are buried in leaves by the forest animals. Here subtle detailing of the children's shoes, just visible beneath the blanket of leaves, and the effective use of white spaces around the animals give a sense of isolation, making this one of Caldecott's most endearing illustrations. This drawing was printed in brown ink, a technique considered by some of Caldecott's contemporaries to be a mere fad. Caldecott, on the other hand, recommended it to Kate Greenaway.

Cover illustration, *The Three Jovial Huntsmen* (1880)

The illustrations to Caldecott's third series of Picture Books, published just after his marriage, were done while working at Henry Blackburn's country home, Farnham Royal, Buckinghamshire. The book was divided into full-page colour plates sandwiched between pages of delicate sketches and text printed in brown ink. Beatrix Potter's father bought the set of original drawings to the book for £80 (cf. Linder, *Journal of Beatrix Potter*, 1966).

'They hunted, an' they hollo'd, an' the first thing they did find
Was a tatter't boggart, in a field, an' that they left behind.'

The Three Jovial Huntsmen (1880)

The book describes the rambles of three men on horseback and the various obstacles they encounter in the countryside. Caldecott adopted the theme for an oil painting which was exhibited at the Royal Academy in 1878 and for a bronze relief which is reproduced here.

'They hunted, an' they hollo'd, an' the next thing they did find
Was a fat pig smiling in a ditch, an' that they left behind.'

The Three Jovial Huntsmen (1880)

Caldecott drew many examples of pigs, which were included in work for the *Graphic, John Gilpin* and *Hey Diddle Diddle,* as a study for the statuette *A Pig in Brittany,* and for a bronze bas-relief, *A Boar Hunt* (1876).

Three Jovial Huntsmen
By permission of the Harvard College Library. Bas-relief, bronze

This relief was probably done after the oil painting *The Three Huntsmen,* and correlates with illustrations to the Picture Book. The preliminary plaster and wax versions were exhibited at the Brasenose Club, Manchester in 1888.

There were Three Ravens Sat on a Tree
By permission of the Harvard College Library. Oil painting

This painting was exhibited at the Royal Academy in 1876.

Cover illustration, *Sing a Song for Sixpence* (1880)

The popular nursery rhyme was published in two earlier versions by Walter Crane, *The Song of Sixpence* (Massé, 1865) and *Aunt Louisa's Sing a Song of Sixpence* (Spencer, 1866), while Caldecott's version added the final optimistic couplet on the fate of the maid's nose, 'But there came a Jenny Wren and popped it on again'. Blackbirds were often used by Caldecott as subjects for paintings in periodicals and book illustrations, including four plates for Mrs. Locker's *What the Blackbird Said* (1881). Illustrations to this and other Picture Books were reproduced by Frederick Warne on handcoloured glass transparencies.

Frontispiece, *Sing a Song for Sixpence* (1880)

The children in Regency costume are an indication of Kate Greenaway's influence on Caldecott. He described her first book *Under the Window* (1878) to Frederick Locker as 'a pretty book' after he had seen the original drawings; later he wrote of his concern that the book was to be 'a guinea book' which he felt would be too expensive.

'The Queen was in the parlour eating bread and honey', *Sing a Song for Sixpence* (1880)

The child model was the grand-daughter of Caldecott's friend and patron, A. J. Mundella, President of the Board of Trade (1886) who wrote, 'My little grand-daughter (Millais' "Dorothy Thorpe") was his model for several of his Christmas books. She is the little girl in *Sing a Song for Sixpence* and several others and possesses copies sent by him with little sketches and dedications' (cf. Blackburn, *Randolph Caldecott,* 1886, pp. 166-8).

Cover illustration, *The Queen of Hearts* (1881)

Caldecott sent the original drawings for this book to the London Fine Arts Society in the summer of 1882, to be sold as a set. His colleague Walter Crane had published the 'The Queen of Hearts' theme as a wallpaper in 1875.

Frontispiece, *The Queen of Hearts* (1881)

Caldecott wrote to a friend on the significance of royalty on playing cards, 'The cards are only dummies & the fact that the mind only contemplates the cardly Kings & queens as dummies & that people play with Kings & queens—throw them away sometimes, put their aces on them indeed may perhaps induce to a properer (sic) estimate of human majesty than if Kings & queens were sent into exile by some families & sympathized with & brought back & fire-sidely nourished by others. Besides there is a significance in having a knave always handy—next in succession....But as the knave never upsets the king or queen—perhaps the Royalists might use this fact of an omnipresent but never supreme knave as an argument in the favour of their sway. The selection of substitutes would be difficult. The monosyllabic names now in use 'ace, king, qe' (sic) are good in that respect. I fear that those who play cards most would prefer royalty' (Harvard letter 24 May 1879).

'The King of Hearts called for those Tarts', *The Queen of Hearts* (1881)

'And Vowed he'd steal no more', *The Queen of Hearts* (1881)

Cover illustration, *The Farmer's Boy* (1881)

Caldecott was aware that his designs were so subtle that even the slightest mark could destroy their delicacy. Here he signed his initials in red on the sheep's back, but in a letter, possibly to the engraver J. D. Cooper, he explained, 'You may think me too particular about this, as for myself I would rather leave out my initials than have them interfere with the drawing—& often do so—& in these slight drawings every little tells. . . .' (Harvard letter 15 August 1877).

Feeding the Calves
By permission of the Harvard College Library. Plaster bas-relief

The country theme in *The Milkmaid* and *The Farmer's Boy* was adopted for this relief. A copy is also owned by the Victoria and Albert Museum, London.

Cover illustration, *The Milkmaid* (1882)

Caldecott sent copies of drawings for the early Picture Books to his friend and respected advisor Frederick Locker, to whom he wrote in 1882, the year this book was published, '*Your* remarks on the last Picture Books, however, are more thoroughly enjoyed & are more useful to me—except perhaps in the way you flatter me. But you shall have a larger book at the end of the year—. . . . I am not sending the books round this time—I feel afraid of seeming to obtrude my bits of pictures on people. It is seldom quite agreeable to me to "show" my attempts at the humorous or beautiful' (Harvard letter 23 October 1882).

(right)
The Babes in the Wood (1879)

Edmund Evans used sharp brown outlines and deep earth-toned colours in this, one of his most successful attempts to recreate Caldecott's original watercolour designs. Here the two children wander alone in the forest, abandoned by their ruffian captors who had argued and fought, one killing the other.

' "Nobody asked you, sir!" she said', *The Milkmaid* (1882)

(left)
'All on a Summer's Day', *The Queen of Hearts* (1881)

This is an example of Caldecott's most brilliant use of colour and detailing, as he recognised in a letter to Frederick Locker, 'As to the QUEEN of Hearts, I am hesitating about making a shilling Picture Book like my last of it, or making a more decorative & complete thing of it (in the future)—introducing the various Kings, Queens, Knaves & their little games & costumes: This between ourselves' (Harvard letter 3 February 1881).

'The little Dog laughed to see such fun', *Hey Diddle Diddle* (1882)

This Picture Book was unique for combining two series of rhymes, *Bye, Baby Bunting* and *Hey Diddle Diddle,* in one volume. The illustrations were printed from clear, simple lines and subtle figure expressions backed against pure, even tones of blue and yellow with red for details.

(opposite top)
'A Lady said to her Son—
a poor young squire
You must seek a Wife with
a Fortune!'

Frontispiece, *The Milkmaid* (1882)

The story tells of a young squire's attempts to marry a milkmaid who rejects him. With the help of her friends she places him atop a wild bull which he rides off into the distance. The engraved version shows the slight alterations Edmund Evans made from Caldecott's original watercolour drawing, *The Interview* (opposite), which is owned by the Manchester City Art Gallery.

Bye, Baby Bunting (1882)

The story tells in rhyming verse how a father shoots a rabbit for his baby's coat—'Gone to fetch a Rabbit skin, To wrap the Baby Bunting in'—and ends with the ironic full-page sketch of the baby dressed in rabbit skin toddling past a group of curious rabbits. Caldecott re-used the group of rabbits or hares in several illustrations (cf. appendix, *The Pictorial World*, *The English Illustrated Magazine*).

Cover illustration, *The Fox Jumps over the Parson's Gate* (1883)

As Beatrix Potter explained in her diary, her father tried to purchase the last coloured sketch for this book but, as was his policy, Caldecott would not allow the drawings to be sold separately. The complete set eventually sold for £90.

The Fox Jumps over the Parson's Gate (1883)

The verse was thought to be one which Caldecott heard on his frequent country walks or while riding his favourite horse. The book ends with a characteristic piece of humour—a brief brown ink sketch of the fox riding a horse chasing a figure running off in the distance. Caldecott adapted scenes for this and other Picture Books from his knowledge of his childhood home. 'Malpas Church, which occupies the summit of a gentle hill some six miles from Whitchurch, occurs frequently as in a full-page drawing in the *Graphic* newspaper....in *Babes in the Wood,* p. 19, in *Baby Bunting,* p. 20, and in the *Fox Jumps over the Parson's Gate,* p. 5' (Blackburn, *Randolph Caldecott,* 1886, p. 208).

Title illustration, *A Frog he would a-wooing go* (1883)

Caldecott made quick brush and ink drawings for the animals to maintain the spontaneity associated with
them. He would often study and make drawings from live specimens and from skeletons, stuffed animals
and casts in the British Museum to determine the proper gestures of his animals.

A Frog he would a-wooing go (1883)

The peacock feather over the gilt frame, emblem of the Aesthetic Movement, recalls the fact that
Caldecott's books were published concurrent with the early career of the movement's chief prophet, Oscar
Wilde, who had just returned from America the year this book was published.

'But as Froggy was crossing a silvery brook,
Heigho, says Rowley!
A lily-white Duck came and gobbled him up,
With a rowley-powley, gammon and spinach,
Heigho, says Anthony Rowley!'

A Frog he would a-wooing go (1883)

A Frog he would a-wooing go
Manchester, City Art Gallery. Brush and ink sketch

Beatrix Potter owned two of these brief brush sketches.

Hares and Frogs
Manchester, City Art Gallery. Watercolour

This small watercolour painting is similar to the engraved illustration, 'The Hares and the Frogs—the Fable', an excerpted series from the book *Fables from Aesop* (1883) which appeared in *The English Illustrated Magazine,* 1883, p. 228 (cf. appendix).

Cover illustration, *Ride a Cock Horse to Banbury Cross* and *A Farmer went Trotting upon his Grey Mare* (1884)

To 'ride a cock horse' usually referred to straddling a toy horse or an adult's knee. Caldecott first used the theme in a full-page colour plate to *Routledge's Christmas Number 1881* (cf. appendix).

'A Raven cried, ''croak!'' and they all tumbled down;
Bumpety, bumpety, bump!
The Mare broke her knees, & the Farmer his crown
Lumpety, lumpety, lump.'

A Farmer went Trotting upon his Grey Mare (1884)

'The mischievous Raven flew laughing away;
Bumpety, bumpety, bump!
And vowed he would serve them the same the next day
Lumpety, lumpety, lump.'

A Farmer went Trotting upon his Grey Mare (1884)

Caldecott drew from much of the landscape surrounding his Farnham, Surrey home from 1882 which he used in the backgrounds of his Picture Books. When he decided to sell the house in 1885 he declared to Frederick Locker, 'There are many objects, views, bits of building in landscape, besides beasts and birds, which have been so handy to my sketchbook that I have neglected them. Some of these I must seize upon before it is too late—so that I intend to be very busy as long as we are here. One or two old ladies have begged that I will not forget to introduce certain ''bits'' of this neighbourhood in future ''Picture Books'' ....' (Harvard letter 10 July 1885).

Cover illustration, *An Elegy on the Glory of her Sex—Mrs. Mary Blaize* by Oliver Goldsmith (1885)

Austin Dobson, an expert on eighteenth-century literature and author of Goldsmith's biography (1888), wrote that Caldecott's charm lay in his ability to take a familiar story like Mary Blaize and twist the details for humour. 'Who, for example, ever before conceived of Madame Blaize as a pawnbroker, because—"She freely lent to all the poor—Who left a pledge behind"?' (preface, *The Complete Collection of Randolph Caldecott's Pictures and Songs,* 1887).

(opposite top)
Cover illustration, *Come Lasses and Lads* (1884)

This popular Picture Book is based on the celebration of May Day, with colour illustrations depicting a country fête. Arthur Locker, editor of the *Graphic* in 1888, interpreted Caldecott's country figures, 'Then how especially charming are his girls! And they are the best type of English girls. Healthy, innocent, yet refined creatures, who keep good hours, and spend much time in the open air. He is less kind to his own sex. Not unfrequently they are ugly, or at all events queer-looking, yet, if he pleases, he can draw the very beau ideal of a manly yet unassuming young Englishman' (preface to the *Complete Collection of R. Caldecott's Contributions to the 'Graphic',* 1888).

(opposite bottom)
May Day
Manchester, City Art Gallery. Oil on cardboard

Based on the same theme as the Picture Book, this painting was exhibited at the Royal Manchester Institution in 1884. Caldecott also painted an oil version on the theme of *Come Lasses and Lads* (cf. Estate catalogue no. 176).

'At church, in silks and satins view with hope of monstrous size,
She never slumbered in her pew.'

An Elegy on the Glory of her Sex—Mrs. Mary Blaize (1885)

Goldsmith's story tells of the last days of a local harlot who is ignored by all but the male population of the village which includes the king. Goldsmith's work was popular with the Victorians—an earlier edition of the *Poems of Oliver Goldsmith* (1859) was published by George Routledge with illustrations by Birket Foster and engraved in six colours by Caldecott's engraver, Edmund Evans.

(right)
The Farmer's Boy
Manchester, Whitworth Art Gallery. Pen, ink and watercolour

An original design to the Picture Book (facing p. 30), this work depicts the poem's last line, 'Says I, My pretty lass, will you come to the banks of the Aire, oh?' Caldecott's friend Frederick Locker wrote a tribute to his country figures, 'He had a delicate fancy, and his humour was as racy as it was refined. He had a keen sense of beauty, and, to sum up all, he had charm. His old world youths and maidens were perfect. The men are so simple and manly, the maidens are so modest and so trustful . . . .' (Blackburn, *Randolph Caldecott,* 1886, p. 207).

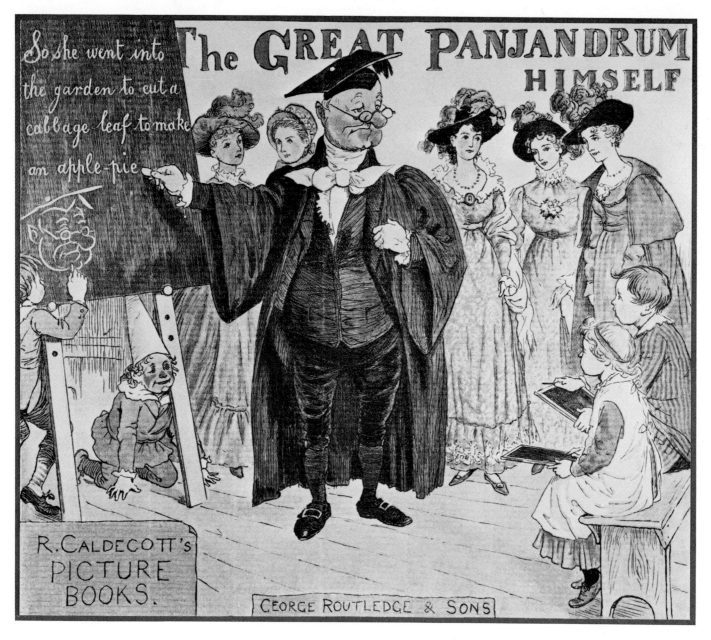

Cover illustration, *The Great Panjandrum Himself* (1885)

Caldecott's last Picture Book was his strangest, a near surreal fantasy which presented a curious number of eighteenth-century personalities including the Great Panjandrum, a satirised academic. Austin Dobson exclaimed, 'And where else had the world been shewn the authentic academic presence—the very "form and pressure"—of the "Great Panjandrum Himself"?' (preface, *The Complete Collection of Randolph Caldecott's Pictures and Songs,* 1887)

(left)
The Farmer's Boy (1881)

Evans' colour illustrations for this Picture Book show the influence of the arcadian landscape tradition; the warm blue-green grass melts into pale orange and pink skies, while the book's rural theme recalls Caldecott's childhood experiences near Whitchurch. The delightfully expressive pigs were first used in *The Three Jovial Huntsmen* (1880).

'. . . .and at the same time a great she-bear coming down the street, pops its head into the shop', *The Great Panjandrum Himself* (1885)

Caldecott received many letters from admirers who felt they knew the inspiration for such settings. Here 'the main street of Whitchurch is fairly pictured'.

'And the Great Panjandrum himself, with the little round button at top. . . .', *The Great Panjandrum Himself* (1885)

'. . . .and they all fell to playing the game of catch-as-catch can, till the gunpowder ran out at the heels of their boots', *The Great Panjandrum Himself* (1885)

'The Toy Country', plate and cover illustration to *The Harz Mountains: A Tour in Toy Country* (1873)

This drawing, which Caldecott made before visiting Germany with Henry Blackburn, suggested the book's eventual title and was embossed in gold upon the cover. He was 26 when, in the autumn of 1872, he made his first visit to the Continent and described one of his many adventures while sketching the local scenery and people. 'Since I saw you I have been wandering in many lands—on mountains, down mines, in secluded vales, & in crowded towns. Once (here I must whisper & impose secrecy), once I was with an English literary man [Blackburn] (with whom & his wife I travelled to many places), well, once I was with him as the evening closed on the ancient town of Blankenburg & we walked continuously along the streets of that usually quiet little place. A fair was being held, many persons were assembled, numberless cake stalls obtruded their wares on our foreign tastes, thousands of toys stared at us, loads of apparel invited us. Sometimes we bought, but on we went & at length we were opposite to a strange mechanical contrivance. We disbursed coin of the realm, we ascended from the ground, we sat aloft in security, strains of soul-stirring music thrilled through our very bones, with no power of our own we began to move, we went faster, faster, and faster, we clove (sic) the air, we whirled round and round, we were galloping on wooden hobby-horses!' (anonymous Harvard letter n.d.).

 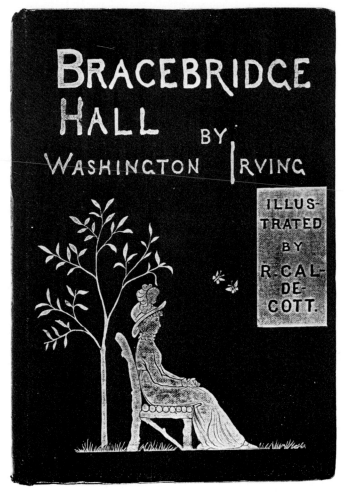

(left)
Original binding, *Old Christmas: from the Sketchbook of Washington Irving* (1876)
London, Victoria and Albert Museum

Old Christmas was published by Macmillan & Co. in a dark green binding with gold embossed design by Caldecott, uniform with *Bracebridge Hall* (1877), and set standards for the binding of later editions of Hugh Thomson's illustrated works in the 1890s. It was published the same year Macmillan issued an illustrated edition of Christina Rossetti's *Goblin Market,* with plates by Dante Gabriel Rossetti and two novels illustrated by Walter Crane. This copy of *Old Christmas* was presented to the Victoria and Albert Museum by Queen Mary.

(right)
Original binding, *Bracebridge Hall* (1877)

(opposite bottom)
Pont-Aven
Manchester, City Art Gallery. Pen and ink sketch

This original sketch was one of the 170 illustrations to *Breton Folk* (1880), facing p. 130. Caldecott wrote his impressions of the scene, 'On approaching Pont-Aven the traveller notices a curious noise rising from the ground and from the woods around him. It is the flickering of the paint brushes on the canvases of the hardworking painters who come into view on leafy nooks and shady corners. These artists go not far from the town where is cider, billiards and tobacco' (cf. Blackburn, *Randolph Caldecott,* 1886, p. 180). The hotel in the distance was supported principally by American artists although many French and English painters stayed there including, in 1888, Caldecott's admirers Gauguin and Van Gogh. This drawing was owned by Beatrix Potter.

On the Road to Market
Manchester, City Art Gallery. Pen and ink drawing

A preliminary sketch for plate facing p. 82, *Breton Folk* (1880), this drawing was originally owned by
Beatrix Potter and was reproduced in *The Christmas Card Sketchbook,* c. 1886, p. 2.

'The Meeting:
On the Way to Cover'

'The Riding:
Now for Glory—Giving the Lady a Lead at the Brook'

'The Fighting:
Love, Disappointment, Jealousy, Rage, Mud and Water'

'The Parting:
Au Revoir'

'The Rivals', series of four colour plates from the *Graphic,* December 1879

Caldecott filled the pages of the *Graphic, Punch* and *The Pictorial World* with such sporting scenes, and gained inspiration from his own love of horse riding and the hunt. He wrote to his then new friend Frederick Locker in 1878, 'I hope you like sporting associations—I have a great liking for a right down good sportsman' (Harvard letter 22 August 1878). He illustrated the letter with a margin sketch of a hunter in tweeds with a dog at his feet. Later he wrote and illustrated an article, 'Fox-hunting: By a Man in a Round Hat', based on his love for the sport, claiming, '. . . .it is better. . . .to make the best of it by revelling in the aspect and emotions of foxhunting as it now affects us than to indulge in glooming (sic) forebodings of evil days or than to try to reconcile the social, political, and sporting sides of the question' (*The English Illustrated Magazine,* 1886, p. 415).

Cover illustration, *Graphic* Christmas Number, 1880

Caldecott wrote to Mrs Locker in March 1880 concerning the pressure of work just before his marriage when he was trying to complete the first Picture Books. 'The *Graphic* people are waiting for two pages for their Xmas No. from me. I fear that I must ask them to persuade themselves that the public can do without me for once' (Harvard letter 5 March 1880). He did, however, publish two pages of six colour sketches to 'The Wynchdale Steeplechase' in the same issue. He wrote to Frederick Locker, 'The *Graphic* Xmas Number 2 pages by me would have been better in more tints: but when I made the drawings I was told that I was too late for several colours. . . .' (Harvard letter 24 November 1880). Indeed, he found one of the most disconcerting aspects of illustrating for annuals was having to draw winter scenes in the spring and summer to allow time for their printing.

'Winter with Us (From our Ironical Artist at Cannes)'

'Winter with You (From our Ironical Artist at Cannes)'

Punch Almanack for 1879, pp. 4-5

Caldecott made these drawings while wintering for his health at the Hotel Gray et d'Albion, Cannes in 1878, where he wrote to William Clough, 'Some blackguard has been intimating in Punch's Almanack—which I don't think a very great one this time—that the weather here is always fine. I believe it usually is. I believe that the moon slides gracefully through a summery sky—in most Xmas days & that the cockrobin would go on piping from the palm trees verdant branch if he didn't happen to have been stalked & slain for food long long ago....The said blackguard's drawings have lost much from reproduction & printing I hear it said in the billiard-room here' (Harvard letter 13 December 1878).

'At a Fancy Ball in the Palazzo Violini he shone with true British lustre'
'Mr. Oakball's Winter in Florence', story with colour illustrations from the *Graphic,* December 1882

Caldecott's story of the ageing bachelor Mr. Oakball, sent to Florence by his mother to overcome low spirits and improve his appetite, has a familiarity to his own life. He in fact visited Florence in the spring of 1879, aged thirty-five, where he wrote a melancholy letter to William Etches, 'Think of me sometimes leaning with pensive cheek upon bony hand gazing over the blue sea or running an enquiring eye over the ruins of Caesar's wine vaults—& sometimes fondling the soft long ears of a melancholy ass which bears a fair, straw-hatted & parasoled burden on some hilly excursion. I'm getting an old fogy now, Will! People put their daughters & nieces under my charge for walks in romantic valleys or for prowls on promenades to view fireworks' (Harvard letter 3 April 1879).

'On the Way Out—"A big Steamer like this never Rolls" ', 'American Facts and Fancies I', *Graphic,*
February-June 1886

Caldecott wrote to Frederick Locker upon his arrival in Philadelphia, 'We met head winds & got the skirts
of some stormy weather which delayed other steamers. Ours was a day late. Mrs. C. was not very well. I
was not seasick at all; but was a little light-headed & lost some rest. I felt the confinement of the cabin for
a day or two, & hated the plunging of the remorseless resistless vessel. There was no getting off. We hope
there will be an overland route discovered by the time of our return' (Harvard letter 18 November 1885).
Like his contemporary Arthur Boyd Houghton, who produced the 'Graphic America' series (1870-2),
Caldecott planned to record the sights and life there while travelling from New York through the South, to
California and back. He arrived in 1885, but his visit was cut short when he died in Florida in February
1886.

'A Quiet Rubber at Whist', 'Facts and Fancies No. 2', *Graphic,* May 1883-June 1884

Caldecott, like his friend George Du Maurier, was a satirist of the leisure hours of the Victorian middle classes. The *Graphic* periodical provided the outlet for his sketched observations made during frequent visits to hotels and casinos in London and on the French Riviera, where he went for his poor health. Here, in particular, he captured the antics of fellow expatriots, American tourists and French locals and sent back in illustrated letters a unique form of pictorial journalism, so popular that the illustrations were reprinted in four separate volumes (cf. appendix).

'Our Artist's Notes at the Royal Agricultural Show at Liverpool', *Graphic,* July 1877

Caldecott's early sketches as reporter-illustrator for the *Graphic, The Pictorial World,* and *London Society* were often tinged with satiric bitterness aimed at the overfed middle classes, perhaps stemming from his sheltered, rural background in the north of England. When sent to record large public gatherings—elections, trials, races—he soon recognised the importance of observing details of the human character and condition. Although he was not a religious man, he wrote to a Mr. Jones in 1873 during these early days in London that '....clowns are very sad men, & I am sad sometimes. The wickedness & frivolity which surround me are fruitful themes for the philosophic pen & the cogitative ink' (Harvard letter 14 October 1873). The letter was headed with a sketch of a clown, with hoardings reading, 'To be seen alive at 46 Gt. Russell St. London [his lodgings]. Great Attraction. Come Early....Babies in arm double price'.

'An English Agricultural Station. The Manure Nuisance at a Country Railway Station', *Graphic,* June 1886

This picture carried the following caption:
'Owing to the modern facilities of transit, manure, for farm and garden operations, is brought from much longer distances than it used to be, and now and then, at country stations there is a regular Bank of Deposit of this valuable but malodorous compost. I chanced to be on the platform once when a fresh load had arrived. The scent was overwhelming, hands instinctively sought noses, and the result, as far as I was concerned, was the above sketch.'

'Afternoon in the King's Road', 'Brighton' series, *Graphic,* December 1879

Arthur Locker, editor of the *Graphic,* wrote in his preface to the *Complete Collection of Randolph Caldecott's Contributions to the 'Graphic'* (1888), 'Lastly, on looking over these fascinating pages, one cannot help observing what a varied gallery of portraits they contain. Some artists contract the habit of reproducing over and over again one familiar type of face. But Caldecott, like Nature, is royally diverse. As a sample of the variety of his types, examine the scores of ladies who are critically inspecting the gentlemen marching along the pier....'

Intense & searching students of Nature

'Intense and searching students of nature', *A Sketchbook of R. Caldecott's* (1873)

Caldecott drew from nature surrounding his country retreats at Kemsing and Farnham, but while in London he learned to use models, as he explained to his early friend John Lennox in a letter asking for a pair of riding breeches, 'I am making a large hunting drawing, & I must draw part from the living model. I want a pair of breeches to draw from. I can get some here, but they won't do' (Harvard letter 21 January 1874). Here he parodies his rival illustrator's work in the Greenaway-inspired costume.

(opposite top)
Cover illustration, *Hey Diddle Diddle* (1882)

Shortly after this book was published Caldecott received a letter from a violin collector, W. Heron Allen, containing the following unusual request, 'I have just seen your new work "Hey diddle diddle". . . . will you allow me to say as a violin collector & connoisseur, that this is the first time I have ever seen a violin reproduced in a frivolous picture, whose proportions and details are scientifically correct. I am just producing a work on the violin, will you give me your permission to reproduce in vignette on the back of my title page the cat & fiddle which forms part of your title cover. . . . I consider that the representation ought to be perpetuated as something more than the title cover of a picture book' (Harvard letter 23 October 1882). Caldecott sent this letter to Frederick Locker with the quip, 'The above is a kind of compliment which I really appreciate, because it evidently comes from a severe sort of man.'

(opposite bottom)
'And the Dish ran away with the Spoon', *Hey Diddle Diddle* (1882)

Kate Greenaway particularly admired this illustration when shown the original drawings for the book at Edmund Evans' office. she wrote to Frederick Locker, 'I've been to call on the Caldecotts today with Mrs. Evans. My brother showed some of his new drawings yesterday at Racquet Court. They are uncommonly clever. The Dish running away with the spoon—you can't imagine how much he has made of it. I wish I had such a mind. I'm feeling very low about my own powers just now. . . .'(Spielmann and Layard, *Kate Greenaway,* 1905, p. 235).

(overleaf)
The Girl I Left Behind Me
Manchester, City Art Gallery. Oil on panel

This is one of Caldecott's more successful paintings in which he used the oil medium perfected while working for Thomas Armstrong, painting birds onto canvas panels for wall decorations. The painting was exhibited at the Royal Manchester Institution in 1896 and at the Manchester Jubilee in 1887 following its sale to Agnews in 1886 for £106 and 1 shilling.

Appendices

BOOKS:

Note: The following list of Caldecott's book illustrations was compiled from catalogues in the British Library (BM), National Union Catalogue (NU), publishers' catalogues such as Macmillan & Co. (Mac), lists in Percy Muir's *Victorian Illustrated Books* (1971) (PM), catalogues in the library and print room of the Victorian and Albert Museum, London (VAM), catalogue of the Parker Collection, Houghton Library, Harvard University, Cambridge, Massachusetts (P), and materials found in the John Johnson collection in the Bodleian library of Oxford University (JJ). Discrepancies in dating are given with the appropriate abbreviations.

BOOKS ILLUSTRATED BY CALDECOTT

1873
The Harz Mountains: A Tour in the Toy Country by Henry Blackburn
London: Sampson Low, Marston, Low & Searle
40 illustrations by Caldecott, Henry Blackburn, Hubert Herkomer and others (cover illustration, 24 sketches and 3 full-page illustrations by Caldecott)

1873
Frank Mildmay or The Naval Officer by Captain Marryat, with a Memoir by Florence Marryat
London and New York: George Routledge & Sons
6 full-page black and white illustrations by Caldecott engraved by Edmund Evans; a little known Caldecott work

1875 (BM)
Baron Bruno or The Unbelieving Philosopher and other Fairy Stories by Louisa Morgan
London: Macmillan & Co.
8 black and white illustrations by Caldecott

1875(M) 1876(BM)
Old Christmas: From the Sketch Book of Washington Irving
London: Macmillan & Co.
120 black and white illustrations by Caldecott, arranged and engraved by J. D. Cooper (First published October 1875; reprinted December 1875; reprinted 1877; second edition 1882; third edition 1886; new edition combined with *Bracebridge Hall* 1886; fourth edition 1892; reissued by Macmillan in a People's Edition with *Bracebridge Hall, Tom Brown's School Days, Wanderings in South America,* one volume, 1882 (Mac))

1877 (BM)
Bracebridge Hall by Washington Irving
London: Macmillan & Co.
116 black and white illustrations by Caldecott, arranged and engraved by J. D. Cooper (First published 1876, dated 1877; reprinted 1877; second edition 1882; third edition with electrotype illustrations 1887 (Mac); large format magazine edition c.1882 (dated by advertisement) with 48 pages, all illustrations and text, priced sixpence, cf. (J.J.) collection)

1878 (BM)
North Italian Folk, Sketches of Town and Country Life by Mrs. Comyns Carr.
London: Chatto and Windus
10 full-page, 18 half-page black and white illustrations by Caldecott (Limited edition of 400 copies London: Pickering and Chatto with 28 hand-coloured plates engraved by Swain; American limited edition New York: Scribner & Welford)

1878
Randolph Caldecott's Picture Books, 16 parts
London: George Routledge & Sons
(Caldecott illustrated 2 per year published in pairs, engraved and printed in colours by Edmund Evans with sewn stiff card covers measuring 9 × 8 inches, each priced one shilling)

1878
The House that Jack Built; The Diverting History of John Gilpin

1879
Elegy on the Death of a Mad Dog by Oliver Goldsmith; *The Babes in the Wood*

1880
Sing a Song for Sixpence; The Three Jovial Huntsmen

1881
The Farmer's Boy; The Queen of Hearts

1882
The Milkmaid; Hey Diddle Diddle and *Bye, Baby Bunting*

1883
A Frog he would a-wooing go; The Fox Jumps over the Parson's Gate

1884
Come Lasses and Lads; Ride a Cock Horse to Banbury Cross and *A Farmer went trotting upon his Grey Mare*

1885
An Elegy on the Glory of her Sex, Mrs. Mary Blaize by Oliver Goldsmith; *The Great Panjandrum Himself*

[1879] (BM)
R. Caldecott's Picture Book: Volume 1
London: George Routledge & Sons
(Reissue of first 4 titles listed above)

[1881] (BM)
R. Caldecott's Picture Book: Volume 2
London: George Routledge & Sons
(Reissue of second 4 titles listed above)

[1881] (BM) 1883 (PM)
R. Caldecott's Collection of Pictures and Songs
London: George Routledge and Sons
(Reissue of above Volumes 1 and 2 in a single volume; reissued London: Frederick Warne [1896] (BM))

[1883] (BM)
The Hey Diddle Diddle Picture Book
London: George Routledge and Sons
(Reissue of third 4 titles listed above)

[1885] (BM)
The Panjandrum Picture Book
London: George Routledge & Sons
(Reissue of last 4 titles listed above)

1885 (PM) [1895] (BM)
R. Caldecott's Second Collection of Pictures and Songs
London: George Routledge and Sons
(Reissue of *The Hey Diddle Diddle Picture Book* and *The Panjandrum Picture Book* in a single volume)

1887 (VAM)
The Complete Collection of Randolph Caldecott's Pictures and Songs, with preface by Austin Dobson
London and New York: George Routledge & Sons
(Limited edition of 800 copies, all 16 Picture Books in single volume, engraved, printed and signed by Edmund Evans)

[1906,7] (BM)
Miniature Picture Books
London and New York: Frederick Warne
(Miniature editions of each title; 4 volumes of 4 titles each were also published)

* * *

1880 (BM)
Breton Folk. An Artistic Tour in Brittany by Henry Blackburn
London: Sampson Low, Marston, Searle & Rivington
170 black and white illustrations by Caldecott
(American edition Boston, 1881 (P))

1881
George Routledge & Sons Coloured Catalogue of New Christmas Books
London: George Routledge & Sons
2 full-page colour illustrations from Caldecott's *The Queen of Hearts* and *The Farmer's Boy*

1881
London Lyrics by Frederick Locker Lampson

London: Chiswick Press
Poems first illustrated by Cruikshank 1857, here with Caldecott's black and white frontispiece 'Girl on a Country Road'
(American edition New York: White Stokes & Allen 1886 (P); American limited edition New York: Private Press for the Book Fellows Club 1883 (BM) for which Caldecott did 3 illustrations; only one is signed 'R.C.', 'A Garden Lyric', p. 32; others attributed stylistically are 'The Widow's Mite', p. 17 and 'On an old Muff', p. 40, cf. Blackburn, *Randolph Caldecott*, 1886, p. 165)

1881
What the Blackbird Said. A Story in Four Chirps by Mrs. Frederick Locker
London and New York: George Routledge & Sons
4 full-page black and white illustrations of birds by Caldecott

1881
Factory Folk during the Cotton Famine by Edwin Waugh
Manchester: John Heywood
Vignette title page by Caldecott depicts mother and child seated before a factory; repeated as a title page in *Lancashire Sketches,* Second Series, 1892

1881
Lancashire Sketches. First Series by Edwin Waugh
Manchester: John Heywood
Vignette title page by Caldecott engraved by Watkinson depicts an old man and a young boy with a rake talking over a fence
(Second Series, 1892)

1881
Tufts of Heather by Edwin Waugh
Manchester: John Heywood
Vignette title page by Caldecott depicts young girls with heather gathered in their skirts
(New edition 1882 with vignette title page of mother and child in a field)

1882
Irish Sketches and Miscellany by Edwin Waugh
Manchester: John Heywood
Vignette title page by Caldecott depicts a man seated on a pile of peat, sunset in the distance

1882
Rambles in the Lake Country by Edwin Waugh
Manchester: John Heywood
Vignette title page by Caldecott depicts a man on horseback, a man seated on a stone wall

1882
Scènes humoristiques
Paris: Librarie Hachette & Cie
Frontispiece and colour illustrations from English periodicals by Caldecott
(French edition of 45 pages; another edition *Nouvelles scènes humoristiques,* 1887 (NU), with 35 pages, frontispiece and colour illustrations, cf. (P) collection)

1883
The Chimney Corner by Edwin Waugh
Manchester : John Heywood
Vignette title page by Caldecott engraved by Watkinson depicting 2 men and women talking under a tree

1883
The Limping Pilgrim on His Wanderings by Edwin Waugh
Manchester: John Heywood
Vignette title page by Caldecott depicts an old man seated, a woman offering him a drink

1883
Poems and Songs by Edwin Waugh
Manchester: John Heywood
34 photo-engraved illustrations, 3 by Caldecott: vignette title page engraved by Watkinson depicts a newspaper seller; p. 20 vignette to 'Chirrup' depicts a tramp on a path; p. 153 vignette to title page 'Poems and Songs in Literary English' depicts men and women on a path leading to a factory
(Second edition 1889 (BM))

1883
Rambles in the Lake Country and other Travel Sketches by Edwin Waugh
Manchester: John Heywood
Compilation of Waugh's previous works listed above with 3 Caldecott illustrations: vignette title page reprinted from *Rambles in the Lake Country;* p. 154 'The Tired Pilgrim' reprinted from *The Limping Pilgrim* here made full-page; p. 245 'The Emerald Isle' vignette reprinted from *Irish Sketches* here made half-page
(Another edition 1893 (BM))

1883 [1882] (BM)
Randolph Caldecott's 'Graphic' Pictures
London and New York: George Routledge & Sons
96 pages colour illustrations reprinted from early issues of the *Graphic* by Edmund Evans (pp. 1-80) and Grant & Co. (pp. 81-96)

(Further editions of Caldecott's *Graphic* contributions followed, cf. 1887, 1888, 1889 entries)

1883
The Vicar of Wakefield by Oliver Goldsmith, preface and notes by Austin Dobson
London: Kegan Paul, Tench & Co.
Black and white frontispiece by Caldecott; a little known work

1883 (BM)
Society Novelettes by F. C. Burnand, H. Savile Clark, R. E. Francillon, etc.
London: Vizetelly & Co.
2 volumes illustrated by Linley Sambourne, M. E. Edwards, F. Dadd, Adelaide Claxton, etc.; Volume I included 4 half-page illustrations by Caldecott to the story 'Crossed in Love'

1883
Some of Aesop's Fables with Modern Instances from new Translations by Alfred Caldecott, M.A.
London: Macmillan & Co.
Caldecott's designs engraved by J. D. Cooper
(First published April 1883; reprinted June 1883 (Mac); American limited edition of 50 copies, New York, with hand-coloured illustrations, cf. (P) collection)

[1883] (BM)
A Sketchbook of R. Caldecott's
London and New York: George Routledge & Sons
48 pages of colour illustrations engraved and printed by Edmund Evans, some reprinted from the *Graphic*, cf. periodicals

1883 (VAM) 1884 (BM)
Jackanapes by Juliana Horatia Ewing
London: Society for Promoting Christian Knowledge
17 full-page and small black and white illustrations by Caldecott
(American edition New York: E. & J. B. Young & Co.; (P) collection listed separate American editions, Boston, 1884, 1886; (VAM) catalogue listed number of copies in print: 1884: 34,000; c. 1885: 50,000; c. 1900: 228,000)

[1884] (BM)
Daddy Darwin's Dovecote. A Country Tale by Juliana Horatia Ewing
London: Society for Promoting Christian Knowledge
17 full-page and small illustrations by Caldecott engraved and printed by Edmund Evans
(American edition New York: E. & J. B. Young & Co.; (BM) catalogue listed 40,000 copies in print c. 1885; (P) collection listed a combined edition with *Jackanapes,* Boston, 1886)

1885
Juliana H. Ewing and her Books by H. K. F. Gatty
London: Society for Promoting Christian Knowledge
Cover and small tailpiece designed by Caldecott
(Reprinted article serialised in Mrs. Gatty's *Aunt Judy's Magazine,* cf. periodicals)

1885
Fables de la Fontaine. A Selection with Introduction, Notes and Vocabulary by Louis M. Moriarity
London: Macmillan & Co.
12 small electrotype black and white illustrations by Caldecott
(Reprinted 1887 and 1889 with 24 additional pages)

[1885] (BM)
Lob Lie-by-the-Fire, or The Luck of Lingborough by Juliana Horatia Ewing
London: Society for Promoting Christian Knowledge
4 full-page and 15 small brown illustrations by Caldecott engraved by Edmund Evans
(American edition New York: E. & J. B. Young & Co.)

1886 (BM)
Jack and the Beanstalk. English Hexameters by Hallam Tennyson
London and New York: Macmillan & Co.
70 pages preliminary sketches by Caldecott for the unfinished book, printed in black and white
(First edition published posthumously November 1886; reprinted twice December 1886 (Mac); the (P) collection owns correspondence between Tennyson and Mrs. Caldecott concerning the publication)

[1886] (BM) [1885] (P)
The Owls of Olynn Belfry. A Tale for Children by A. Y. D.
London: Field & Tuer—The Leadenhall Press; C. Simpkin, Marshall & Co.; Hamilton, Adams & Co.
12 full-page and 6 small illustrations by Caldecott

[1886] (P)
A Few Sketches by the Late Randolph Caldecott with Compliments
(Publisher unknown)
8 full-page black and white illustrations from Caldecott's *Breton Folk* in an oblong, string-bound volume 16 inches long with 'Christmas Greeting' printed on the cover, cf. (P) collection

[1886] (P)
The Christmas Card Sketch Book

London: Marion & Co.
24 pages black and white illustrations including 3 by Caldecott: 2 from *Breton Folk*, 1 titled 'Taming of the Shrew—Petrucio takes home his Bride'; others by Walter Crane, Orchardson, H. S. Marks, cf. (P) collection
(American edition Boston: H. Carter & Karrick; French edition Paris: 14 Cité Bergère)

[1887] (BM)
Fascimiles of Original Sketches
Manchester: J. Galloway
16 pages black and white illustrations by Caldecott from *Will o' the Wisp* 1868, cf. periodicals

1887 [1886] (BM)
More 'Graphic' Pictures
London and New York: George Routledge & Sons
71 pages colour illustrations from Caldecott's contributions to the *Graphic*, cf. periodicals

1888 [1887] (BM)
Randolph Caldecott's Last 'Graphic' Pictures
London and New York: George Routledge & Sons
71 pages colour illustrations from Caldecott's later contributions to the *Graphic*, cf. periodicals

1888
The Complete Collection of Randolph Caldecott's Contributions to the 'Graphic', with a preface by Arthur Locker
London and New York: George Routledge & Sons
(Limited edition of 1,250 copies signed by Evans and Routledge, illustrations engraved and printed by Evans from the *Graphic* issues 1876-1886; another edition *Randolph Caldecott's 'Graphic' Pictures. Complete Edition*, London and New York: George Routledge & Sons 1891 (BM), being the 4 'Graphic' volumes listed above in a single volume; another edition in oblong format 1898 (BM))

[1888] 1889 (BM)
Gleanings from the 'Graphic' by Randolph Caldecott
London and New York: George Routledge & Sons
84 pages select colour illustrations compiled from the *Graphic*, cf. periodicals

1888
Catalogue of a Loan Collection of the Works of Randolph Caldecott at the Brasenose Club with memoir by George Evans
Manchester: John Heywood
24 pages black and white illustrations by Caldecott engraved by Watkinson
(Original edition with brown paper cover, darker brown type and pictures; another limited edition of only plates printed for club members, in dark blue on grey and brown paper, cf. (P) collection)

[1889] 1890 (BM)
Randolph Caldecott Sketches with an Introduction by Henry Blackburn
London: Sampson Low & Co.
94 pages black and white illustrations compiled from early sketchbooks and periodicals

1892
Artistic Travel. A Thousand Miles Towards the Sun. Artistic Travel in Normandy, Brittany, the Pyrenees, Spain and Algeria by Henry Blackburn
London: Sampson Low, Marston & Co.
130 black and white illustrations with 33 from Caldecott's *Breton Folk*, although in different sizes from the originals

1894
The Art of Illustration by Henry Blackburn
London: W. H. Allen & Co.
95 black and white illustrations including animal frieze by Caldecott originally reproduced in Blackburn, *Randolph Caldecott*, 1886. p. vii

[1895] (BM)
Randolph Caldecott's Painting Book
London: Society for Promoting Christian Knowledge
(For another separate *Painting Book* cf. 1902 entry)

1897
Sporting Society or Sporting Chat and Sporting Memories edited by Fox Russell
London: Bellairs & Co.
2 volumes with Caldecott's illustrations: Vol. I, frontispiece 'Going to Cover' and 5 full-page illustrations to the story 'Huntingcrop Hall' by Alfred E. T. Watson pp. 268-285; Vol. II, frontispiece 'In Full Cry' depicting a hunting scene

1899 (VAM)
Lightning Sketches for 'The House that Jack Built' introduced by Aubyn Trevor-Battye
London: The 'Artist' in aid of the London hospital
30 preliminary sketches by Caldecott for the Picture Book (cf. 1879 entry) reproduced in brown, photo-zincotypes by Edmund Evans
(American edition New York: Frederick Warne n.d.)

[1902] (BM) [1901] (P)
Randolph Caldecott's Painting Book (First Series)
London and New York: Frederick Warne

1925 (NU)
Jean Gilpin, l'histoire divertissante de la promenade à cheval écrit par William Cowper et francisée par E. Gutch
New York: Frederick A. Stokes
(American edition in French of the Picture Book, cf. 1878 entry)

1942 (NU)
A Christmas Interlude
Chicago: The Cuneo Press
Collection of famous yuletide stories, poems and plays with 32 Caldecott illustrations

(undated) (P)
In a Good Cause
Published for the benefit of the North Eastern Hospital for Children
Frontispiece 'Only a Scratch' by Caldecott

PERIODICALS:

Academy Notes

Illustrations of some of the Principal Pictures at Burlington House, edited by Henry Blackburn from 1875 to 1894.

p. 17: 'Portrait of Captain Richard Burton by Frederick Leighton' (Caldecott made the sketch from memory using a style of heavy cross-hatched line to reproduce the original painting's depth of surface; reproduced from Blackburn, *Randolph Caldecott* (1886), p. 139)

p. 32: 'An Old Poacher by H. H. Couldery' (Caldecott again sketched the painting from memory, here attributed to him on stylistic grounds)

p. 40: 'There were Three Ravens Sat on a Tree' (small sketch by Caldecott after his own painting, Royal Academy, 1876)

p. 55: 'Three Huntsmen riding home in evening light' (listed but not given with a sketch, Caldecott refused to have it reproduced after it was hung disastrously at the Academy so that none of the detail could be seen, Royal Academy, 1878)

Academy Sketches

Established by Henry Blackburn in 1883, included about 200 illustrations after works exhibited at the Royal Academy, Grosvenor Gallery, Institute of Painters in Water Colour, Society of British Artists, etc.

1883, p. 142: 'Putting the Hounds into Cover' (sketch by Caldecott of his race scene; Institute of Painters in Water Colour)

1885, p. 135: 'The First Flight' (sketch by Caldecott of a hunting scene, engraved by Dawson; Institute of Painters in Water Colour)

Aunt Judy's Magazine

Caldecott redesigned the magazine's cover to represent a group of children gathered around an elderly woman reading to them, to be printed in dark brown on pale yellow card similar to the Picture Books.

Annual Volume 1882: Coloured frontispiece 'D'ye see yon chap?' (depicts two elderly gentlemen seated on a stone wall)

February 1883, p. 322: Full-page engraved illustration to the story 'Mother's Birthday Review' by J. H. Ewing (depicts 2 small girls and 2 donkeys; repeated in colour as 'The Spectators' in *A Sketchbook of R. Caldecott's* (1883), p. 16)

p. 325: Full-page engraved illustration (depicts a boy on a horse with 3 boys about to follow; repeated in colour in *A Sketchbook of R. Caldecott's* (1883), p. 13)

Annual Volume 1885, p. 750: Small tailpiece to article 'Juliana Horatia Ewing, Part IV' (depicts child laying wreath on gravestone marked 'J. H. E. May 1885'; repeated as cover to Mrs. Gatty's *Juliana H. Ewing and her Books* (1885), repeated p. 82, cf. book entry)

Belgravia: A London Magazine

Caldecott designed a series of full-page illustrations to the serial 'Lost for Love' by M. E. Braddon, the magazine's editor, each engraved by Edmund Evans.

Volume 22, 1873: Frontispiece 'Mark Chamney' (depicts two men shaking hands in a library)

Facing p. 144: 'The Doctor Makes Amends' (depicts three men and a woman having tea)

Facing p. 273: 'Loo Makes Aquaintance with the Poets' (depicts a man and a woman standing before an artist's easel)

Facing p. 407: 'You Shouldn't Have Done That' (depicts a man and a woman in a carriage)

Volume 23, 1874: Frontispiece 'It was all over' (depicts a man and a woman in a churchyard)

Facing p. 147: 'Waiting for Walter's Return' (depicts two men and woman seated in a drawing room)

Facing p. 278: 'Flora's Visitor' (depicts an elderly lady standing before a young woman)

Facing p. 411: 'Flora on her Sketching Expedition' (depicts a girl walking in a wood)

Volume 24, 1874: Frontispiece 'Mr. Gurner's Unexpected Return' (depicts a middle-aged man entering a room where an elderly lady is having tea)

Facing p. 140: 'Alone Among the Roses' (depicts a woman walking in a garden, holding an umbrella)

Facing p. 271: 'It is only a Likeness' (depicts a woman hiding in a graveyard, watching a man)

Facing p. 399: 'Between Life and Death' (depicts a woman at a man's bedside)

Volume 25, 1875: Frontispiece 'You live only to do good to others' (attributed to Caldecott in the illustration list but labelled 'H. French, del. J. R. Battershell, sc.')

Facing p. 144: 'Jarred Promises Reformation' (depicts a man and a woman walking in a garden at night)

The English Illustrated Magazine

Edited by J. W. Comyns Carr, issued from 1883-1913, published by Macmillan and Co.

Volume I, 1883: 4 full-page drawings engraved by J. D. Cooper to the series 'Fables from Aesop' adopted from the 1883 book (cf. book entry)

p. 228: 'The Hares and the Frogs—the Fable' (depicts hares and frogs near a pond)

p. 229: 'The Hares and the Frogs—the Application' (depicts a group of businessmen deciding on dividends)

p. 288: 'The Kid and the Wolf—the Fable' (depicts a goat on a roof watching the wolf)

p. 289: 'The Kid and the Wolf—Application' (depicts a country court)

pp. 300-305: 5 small illustrations of dogs to Robert Louis Stevenson's article 'The Character of Dogs'

Volume 3, 1885-6: 13 small and full-page illustrations to an article written by Caldecott 'Fox-Hunting: By the Man in a Round Hat'

p. 414: Small drawing 'The Meet'

p. 415: Small drawing 'Some Round-Hats'

p. 416: Small drawings 'At the Covert Side' and 'Gone Away'

p. 417: Full-page drawing 'On the Surrey Common'

p. 418: Small drawing 'Pulling Down a Rail'

p. 419: Small drawings 'At a Gate' and 'Among the Turnips'

p. 420: Full-page drawing 'Fox-Hunting'

p. 421: Small drawing 'Don't Ride over the Snowdrops'

p. 422: Small drawings 'Thrown Out' and 'A Small Farmer'

p. 423: Small untitled hunt scene

Graphic

Caldecott illustrated full pages or series in a number of issues from 1872 to 1886, which were reproduced in four separate volumes and one complete volume (see separate book entries). The following is a complete list of illustrated series.

Autumn 1872: 'Sketches for Harz Mountains'

April 1874: 'The Quorn Hunt' (large single engraving)

December 1876: 'Christmas Visitors' (select illustrations from *Old Christmas*, (1876)); 'Bracebridge Hall by Washington Irving' (select illustrations from *Bracebridge Hall*, (1877))

March-May 1877: 'Letters from Monaco' (series of fictitious letters written and illustrated by Caldecott)

March 1877: 'Sketches at Buxton' (series of sketches made from on-the-spot observations)

July 1877: 'Notes at the Royal Agricultural Show at Liverpool' (full-page series sketches)

December 1877: 'Will Blisson's Last Round' (full-page illustrated story; original drawings owned by Harvard Library)

June 1878: Cover to the *Graphic* Summer Number; 'Mr. Chumley's Holidays' (series over several pages with colour illustrations)

December 1878: Cover to the *Graphic* Christmas Number; 'A Hunting Family' (number of illustrations)

Summer 1879: 'Flirtations in France' (series with colour illustrations depicting English holiday-makers in the south of France)

October 1879: 'Sketches at Trouville' (series of illustrated sepia sketches depicting bathers at Trouville)

December 1879: 'Brighton' (series of sepia sketches depicting aspects of visiting Brighton, including double-page illustrations of promenaders along the King's Road); 'The Rivals' (4 colour illustrations depicting a race between two men for the favour of a woman)

September 1880: 'A Visit to Venice' (series over several pages with handwritten script and illustrations printed in blue)

December 1880: Cover to the *Graphic* Christmas Number; 'The Wynchdale Steeplechase' (series of 2 pages, 6 colour sketches drawn on-the-spot)

Summer 1881: 'Our Haymaking' (series of brown and blue colour sketches depicting a harvest)

December 1881: 'Mr. Carlyon's Christmas' (illustrated story with colour plates throughout the text depicting an eighteenth-century Christmas celebration reminiscent of Caldecott's drawings for *Old Christmas* (1876))

February 1882: 'A Meet on Exmoor' (series of drawings of a hunt)

Summer 1882: 'The Legend of Old Cromer' (illustrated story of amateur landscape painter, with colour plates throughout the text)

December 1882: 'Mr. Oakball's Winter in Florence' (story with colour illustrations depicting an ageing English bachelor sent to Florence for his health)

April 21 1883: 'Leaves from a Sketchbook of R. Caldecott's' (published excerpts from the 1883 sketchbook, cf. book entry)

May 1883-June 1884: 'Facts and Fancies' (series of single-page plates depicting leisure activities of Victorian life at home and abroad)

Summer 1883: 'How Tankerville Smith Took a Country Cottage' (story with colour illustrations throughout the text depicting a bachelor's purchase of a country cottage, suggesting Caldecott's own purchase of Kemsing)

December 1883: 'Diana Wood's Wedding' (story over several pages with colour illustrations)

February 1884: 'Scenes with the old Mickledale Hunt'

June 1884: 'Notes at the Shakespearian Show' (single-page series of sketches)

Summer 1884: 'A Lovers' Quarrel' (series of colour plates depicting man and woman quarrelling while a bull threatens the man's life)

December 1884: 'The Legend of the Laughing Oak' (illustrated story)

Summer 1885: 'The Strange Adventures of a Dog-cart' (illustrated story)

December 1885: 'The Curmudgeon's Christmas' (story over several pages with colour illustrations)

February-June 1886: 'American Facts and Fancies I and II' (part of an uncompleted series of illustrations commissioned when Caldecott went to America; they depict scenes in Washington, and the South, where Caldecott died in February 1886)

February 27, 1886: 'In Memorium—Selections from the drawings of the late Randolph Caldecott contributed at various times to the *Graphic*'

June 1886: 'An English Agricultural Station' (single-page engraving issued posthumously); 'Paul and Virginia' (story with colour illustrations over several pages, depicts marriage and adventures of the two with a band of pirates)

Grosvenor Notes

With Facsimiles of Sketches by the Artists, edited by Henry Blackburn.

1878, p. 57: 'A Boar Hunt' (sketch by Caldecott of his bronze bas-relief)

Harper's New Monthly Magazine

Volume 47, No. 277, June 1873, pp. 67-86: 22 Caldecott sketches from *Harz Mountains* (1873) to accompany an excerpt from the book, published in this New York periodical

Illustrated London News

Volume 39, No. 1120, December 7 1861, p. 578: Half-page engraving 'Destruction by Fire of the Queen Railway Hotel at Chester' (Caldecott's first published illustration included with a first-hand account of the disaster)

London Society

Volume XX, p. 417: Small engraving 'A Debating Society—Clinching an Argument, Sketch at a Debating and Mutual Improvement Society' engraved by J. D. Cooper (reproduced in Blackburn, *Randolph Caldecott* (1886), p. 21)

Volume XXI, p. 17: Small engraving 'It's an ill wind that blows any good' (depicts three figures—Lesbia, Phoebe, young Colin; reproduced in *Randolph Caldecott's Sketches* (1890), p. 14)

p. 80, 275: Series of small engravings 'Scenes from Ensign Rollynge's Christmas in the Jungle' (depicts English officers in India; reproduced in *Randolph Caldecott's Sketches* (1890), p. 33)

Christmas Number 1871: Illustrations to 'The Two Trombones' by F. Robson (comic series where 2 men become entangled in each other's instruments; reproduced in *Randolph Caldecott's Sketches* (1890), p. 28)

September 1872, p. 248-9: Double-page series of comic sketches 'Going out of Town' (depicts the preliminary trials of railway travel)

Christmas Number 1872, p. 16: Half-page engraving to poem 'Artful Creature' by T. H. S. Escott (depicts young girl reading while man watches at the door)

p. 40-1: Double-page series 'King Coal' (depicts the uses of coal in several drawings arranged around a central 'Coal King')

pp. 87-95: Series of small engravings to story 'Huntingcrop Hall' by Alfred E. T. Watson (p. 87 depicts man astride a chair-cum-horse whipping it; p. 90 depicts a man in riding habit watching out a window; p. 93 depicts a man on horseback grabbing at his fallen hat; p. 94 depicts a man lunging forward as his horse rises from a stream; p. 95 depicts a man and a woman riding together)

Christmas Number 1875: 4 illustrations to Irish story 'Philosopher Push' engraved by H. Watkinson (depicts an elderly tramp eating at a table; an old man before a trunk; portrait of a woman; also reproduced in *Brasenose Catalogue* (1888))

The Pictorial World

Volume I, No. 1, March 7 1874, p. 4: Half-column engraving to 'About Politics and Politicians' (depicts several men in various groups, a third column sketch of politicians huddled in a group)

p. 5. Two-third column series of sketches to the 'Close of the Tichborne Trial: Scenes in Westminster': 'Waiting to See the Claimant' (depicts crowds of spectators); 'The Break-up' (depicts men in court room) (also reproduced in Blackburn, *Randolph Caldecott*, (1886), p. 78)

p. 13: Two-third page series of sketches 'Sketches of the Recent Elections' (series of vignettes joined by flowers and ivy branches depicting a polling booth being watched; orators on a speaker's platform; men announcing 'State of the Poll'; a tramp eyeing a ballot box; an Irish politician speaking to a crowd; a 'Home Rule' parody; Scottish Highlanders dashing to the polls; 'a committee')

No. 2, March 14 1874, p. 26: Small sketch to series 'About New Pictures', probably written by the art director Henry Blackburn (attributed to Caldecott stylistically, depicts artist admiring a portrait with an elderly man watching)

No. 3, March 21 1874, p. 46: Quarter-page sketch 'Camden House, Chislehurst, on March 16 1874' (depicts a group of people on a lawn); small sketch 'The Bonapartist Celebration at Chislehurst: on the Lawn at Camden House' (depicts group of spectators presenting violets to a dignitary)

No. 4, March 28 1874, p. 55: 2 small sketches to the article 'How the House Looks' (depicts procession of Speaker of the House and Prime Minister addressing the House; also reproduced in Blackburn, *Randolph Caldecott* (1886), pp. 81, 83)

No. 9, May 1874, p. 132: Half-page drawing 'Somebody's Coming!' (depicts two rabbits, Caldecott's first attributed illustration in a periodical)

No. 14, June 6 1874, p. 216: Small sketch to serial 'About Books' (depicts an old man writing; attributed stylistically to Caldecott)

No. 15, June 13 1874, p. 238: Small sketch to article 'Comments on the Commons by an Honourable Commoner' (depicts a gentleman reading *The Pictorial World*)

No. 20, July 18 1874, p. 346: Full-page engraving 'A Morning Walk drawn by R. Caldecott' (depicts four cranes, also reproduced in *Randolph Caldecott Sketches* (1890), p. 14)

Volume II, No. 32, October 10 1874, p. 120: 4 small sketches to the article 'Sketches in Brittany' by Henry Blackburn (plates taken from *Breton Folk* (1880))

No. 41, December 12 1874 p. 304: Full-page engraving 'Fox Hunting: Gone Away drawn by R. Caldecott' (depicts a hunt with men and women)

No. 50, February 13 1875, p. 477: Half-page series of vignettes 'Valentine Vagaries drawn by R. Caldecott' (depicts series of greeting cards)

No. 54, March 13 1875, p. 31: Small sketch to an anonymous story 'The Origin of Railway Accidents' (depicts farmer and horse cart overturned by a train)

Volume III, No. 71, July 10 1875, p. 319; Small sketch 'Fashionable Foibles' (depicts portrait heads of 8 men in historic costumes reminiscent of the *Graphic* works)

Volume IV, No. 95, Christmas Number, December 25 1875, p. 275: 4 small drawings for the article 'Christmas as Described by Washington Irving' (from Caldecott's sketches for *Old Christmas* (1876))

p. 287: Half-page engraving 'In Vino Veritas': 'O, the mad days I have spent. . . .Oh, the days that we have seen!' Henry IV, Act III, scene 2 (depicts four men seated at a table drinking)

Punch

Volume 62, June 22 1872, p. 255: Small inset drawing 'Chemistry for Countrymen' (depicts a Whitehall guard chasing a boy wearing his fur hat; signed 'R.C.'; also reproduced in Blackburn, *Randolph Caldecott* (1886), p. 31)

Volume 64, January 25 1873, p. 42: Small inset drawing 'The Weather and the Chase' (depicts a hunter seated with dead rabbits at his feet to illustrate an article on H. M.'s staghounds unable to hunt because of inclement weather)

March 8 1873, p. 97: Small inset drawing 'Good Times for Dunces' (depicts school master with cane, a boy cowering behind a blackboard marked 'A School Board'; also reproduced in Blackburn, *Randolph Caldecott* (1886), p. 51)

Almanack for 1879, p. 4, 5: Half-page pair of illustrations: 'Winter for Us (from our Ironical Artist at Cannes)' and 'Winter for You (from our Ironical Artist at Cannes)' (depicts promenading Englishmen on holiday in the south of France, while the companion depicts group battling the windy rain of London, the latter drawn in a curiously similar style to Caldecott's associate Walter Crane)

Volume 76, June 1879, p. 253: Small drawing 'Symptoms of a Bank Holiday' (depicts a gentleman having his shoes polished by an old man)

Volume 77, August 2 1879, p. 47: Half-page drawing 'Not such Disagreeable Weather for the Haymakers as some People Think' (depicts four couples seated on a fence in the rain, hidden under umbrellas; also reproduced in *R. Caldecott's Sketches* (1890), p. 71)

Almanack for 1880, p. 2: Half-page drawing engraved by Swain 'If you don't happen to be a Sporting Man, and are out for a quiet ride, it's very annoying when your horse insists upon joining the Hounds that are running a field or two off the High-road' (depicts a man on horseback jumping a hedge, being watched by a tramp)

p. 3: Half-page drawing engraved by Swain 'And it is not pleasant to be overtaken in a Narrow Lane by a Troop of Hunting People who have been thrown out, and trying hard to catch the Hounds' (depicts an old man on horseback being overtaken by hunters)

p. 12: Half-page drawing 'An Innocent Offender' (depicts a fat gentleman with rose in his lapel being attacked by customs officials at Menton for carrying a plant illegally across the border; the first Caldecott illustration which uses his associate, George Du Maurier's style of social satire)

Volume 83, November 18 1882, p. 239: Half-page drawing 'What's in a Name?', 'Whip, Wisdom! Get away there!! Wisdom! Wisdom! Ugh-you always were the biggest fool in the Pack!' (depicts huntsman and his dogs)

December 16 1882, p. 287: Half-page drawing 'Q.E.D.!' (depicts young man on horseback and old man reading a sign on his back)

p. 288: Half-page parody of Caldecott's Picture Book, *The Milk Maid* (1882) by Harry Furniss, 'Theatrical Nursery Rhyme in the Caldecottian Style' (depicts milk maid as Lily Langtry, her dog as Oscar Wilde)

December 30 1882, p. 303: Half-page parody by Harry Furniss 'Parliamentary Nursery Rhyme in the Caldecottian Style' (depicts the Sergeant at Arms, a beetle, in a sequence after the rhyme Hickory, Dickory, Dock)

Almanack for 1883, p. 20: Full-page engraving by Swain 'Mr. Bibble Hunts the Stag' (depicts series of sketches of a hunt separated by plant branches)

Volume 84, February 10 1883, p. 69: Half-page parody by Harry Furniss 'Royal Musical Collegiate Nursery Rhyme in the Caldecottian Style' (depicts Hey Diddle Diddle theme with theatrical overtones)

Volume 90, February 27 1886, p. 106: 'Randolph Caldecott. In Memorium' (unillustrated full-page poem)

December 6, 1933, n.p: Half-page parody on Caldecott's Picture Book, *The Three Jovial Huntsmen*, 'The Three (Don't-be-too) Jovial Huntsmen', signed B.P. after R.C. (depicts contemporary political figures as huntsmen confronting a cow)

Routledge Christmas Number 1881

p. 2: Half-page illustration to Mrs. Frederick Locker's story, 'Greystoke Hall', pp. 2-6 (depicts a girl on a pony before an old woman)

Facing p. 12: Full-page colour plate 'Ride a Cock Horse to Banbury Cross' (depicts children riding red, yellow and blue-spotted ponies past a village green; the volume also includes colour plates by Walter Crane, Kate Greenaway, and Gustave Doré; priced one shilling)

The Sphinx

Volume II, No. 72, December 25 1869: 2 full-page comic series between pp. 308-9 'The Mistletoe Beau: A New Version of an old Story'; 'Mrs. Bodkins's Christmas Party' (early drawing room comedies styled after John Leech. This paper was another short-lived Manchester periodical (Vol. I, July 25 1868) while Caldecott's 2 illustrations were the first of any pictures to appear in the first 33 numbers of the paper)

Will o' The Wisp

July 1868: Small comic sketch 'Latest Apparition. The Will o' the Wisp' (depicts a young boy with a copy of this new paper with other comic periodicals personified and staring at him in amazement. Caldecott did several sketches for this short-lived Manchester serio-comic paper (which was usually 12 pages long, each issue with double-page centre illustration); these were reproduced in facsimile by J. Galloway in 1887, cf. book entry)

PAINTINGS IN OIL:

Hunting Sketches
Exhibited Royal Manchester Institution, March 1872

At the Coverside
Exhibited Dudley Gallery, no. 196, 1872, price 10 gns.

There were Three Ravens Sat on a Tree
Exhibited Royal Academy, no. 415, 1876; Brasenose Club, no. 127, 1888; owned by Harvard Library; reproduced from a sketch by Caldecott in Henry Blackburn's *Academy Notes*, 1876, p. 40

The Three Huntsmen
Exhibited Royal Academy no. 597, 1878; Manchester Jubilee 1887; originally purchased by Caldecott's friend Mr. Mundella; reproduced *Randolph Caldecott's Sketches*, 1890, p. 70; in the French periodical *L'Art*, Vol XX, p. 211; Blackburn, *Randolph Caldecott*, 1886, p. 167. The estate sale catalogue listed a similar oil painting entitled *The Three Jovial Huntsmen*, no. 175

View from the Palace Gardens, Monaco
Estate sale catalogue, no. 156

Menton: Clothes Drying
Estate sale catalogue, no. 156

Menton: Peasant Girls at a Brook
Estate sale catalogue, no. 157

Italian Cattle
Estate sale catalogue no. 158

Gentle and Simple
Estate sale catalogue, no. 159

A Sketch at Kemsing
Estate sale catalogue, no. 160

Hayfield at Frensham
Estate sale catalogue, no. 161

The Ness, Shaldon, Devon
Estate sale catalogue, no. 162

The Bar, Shaldon Harbour
Estate sale catalogue, no. 163

Kentish Cottages
Estate sale catalogue, no. 164

Hop Pickers
Estate sale catalogue, no. 165

Ploughing
Estate sale catalogue, no. 166

Cows in a Meadow: Kemsing
Estate sale catalogue, no. 167

A Bay Horse
Estate sale catalogue, no. 168

Merrylegs; his Favourite Hunter
Estate sale catalogue, no. 169

Gone Away
Estate sale catalogue, no. 170

The Return Home
Estate sale catalogue, no. 171

Cub-hunting
Estate sale catalogue, no. 172; exhibited Brasenose Club, no. 61, 1888

With the Mid-Kent
Estate sale catalogue, no. 173

Fox-hunting in Surrey
Estate sale catalogue, no. 174

Lasses and Lads
Estate catalogue no. 176

New Shoes
Estate catalogue, no. 177

The Mysterious Lay Figure
Estate sale catalogue, no. 178

The Bouquet
Estate sale catalogue, no. 179

A Lady in Yellow Silk Dress
Estate sale catalogue, no. 180

A Garden Scene with Figures
Estate sale catalogue, no. 181

The Maypole (see also *May Day*)
Estate sale catalogue, no. 182

A Meeting of Shareholder's Declaration of Dividend
Estate sale catalogue, no. 183; exhibited Manchester Jubilee 1887

An Interesting Patient
Estate sale catalogue, no. 184

Volunteers of the Great War
Estate sale catalogue, no. 185

Tea-time
Estate sale catalogue, no. 187

Study of Fancy Dress
Estate sale catalogue, no. 188

Belgian Hares
Estate sale catalogue, no. 189

Poultry
Estate sale catalogue, no. 190

The Recognition
Estate sale catalogue, no. 191

The Court-martial
Estate sale catalogue, no. 192

The Companion
Estate sale catalogue, no. 194

A Flight of Field-fares
A Covey of Partridges
Two panels for decorative interior work; estate sale catalogue, no. 195-6

The Girl I Left Behind Me
Exhibited Royal Manchester Institution, no. 747, 1886; Manchester Jubilee, no. 729, 1887; owned by City Art Gallery, Manchester

May Day
Exhibited Royal Manchester Institution, no 778, 1884; Manchester Jubilee Exhibition, no. 738, 1887; owned by City Art Gallery, Manchester

'Twas the Fiddler Play'd it Wrong
Done in 1884, exhibited Brasenose Club, no. 57, 1888

Evening near Quimperle, Brittany
Exhibited Brasenose Club, no. 58, 1888

Scene at Menton: The Goatherd
Exhibited Brasenose Club, no. 59, 1888

The Volunteer's Courtship
Exhibited Brasenose Club, no.60, 1888

Monaco
Exhibited Brasenose Club, no. 62, 1888

Fruit Dealing, Chioggia
Exhibited Brasenose Club, no. 63, 1888

Italian Figures, Chioggia
Exhibited Brasenose Club, no. 68, 1888

Sir Simon and the Squire Chatting with the Milkmaid
Scene from *Bracebridge Hall*, 1876, p. 87; exhibited Brasenose Club, no. 64, 1888

Cavaliers and Roundheads in a Cabaret at Quimperle
Exhibited Brasenose Club, no. 66, 1888

Mrs. Elizabeth Spencer George
Exhibited Brasenose Club, no. 118, 1888

Three Pelicans and Tortoise
Reproduced in Blackburn, *Randolph Caldecott,* 1886, p. 131

SCULPTURE:

Astrophel, bas-relief in bronze
Exhibited Royal Academy, no. 1591, 1882; Brasenose Club, no. 6, 1888

The Mistletoe, wax model
Exhibited Brasenose Club, no. 12, 1888

Hunting Scene, frieze
Exhibited Brasenose Club, no. 18, 1888

Horse Fair in Brittany, bas-relief in metal
Exhibited Royal Academy, no. 1499, 1876; Brasenose Club, no. 26, 1888;
5 versions of this were listed in the 1886 estate sale catalogue

Feeding the Calves, tinted bas-relief
Exhibited Brasenose Club, no. 29, 1888; copy owned by Harvard Library

A Boar Hunt, bas-relief in bronze
Done in 1876, exhibited Grosvenor Gallery, no. 232, 1878; Brasenose
Club, no. 32, 1888; reproduced in Henry Blackburn's *Grosvenor Notes,*
1878, p. 53; estate sale catalogue listed 3 bronze versions; it is known
Caldecott originally reproduced the relief in limited edition of 6, each sold
for 10 guineas

Huntsmen and Hounds, tinted bas-relief, also bronze version
Both exhibited Brasenose Club, nos. 33, 45, 1888

Girl Feeding Calves, also known as *Feeding Calves,* wax, plaster and
bronze bas-relief
Wax and bronze versions exhibited at the Brasenose Club, nos. 36, 42,
1888; plaster copy owned by Harvard Library

Three Jovial Huntsmen, tinted plaster bas-relief, also bronze version
Both versions exhibited Brasenose Club, nos. 40, 51, 1888; copies in
bronze and wax owned by Harvard Library

Horse Fair, Le Folquet, Brittany, terra-cotta frieze
Exhibited Brasenose Club, no. 47, 1888; wax version done in 1875

The Soldier's Farewell, bas-relief in bronze
Exhibited at Brasenose Club, no. 48, 1888

The Diligence, bas-relief in bronze
Exhibited Brasenose Club, no. 50, 1888; copy owned by Harvard Library

The Tennis Player, plaster statuette
Exhibited Brasenose Club, no. 81, 1888

Mare and Foal, terra-cotta statuette
Exhibited Brasenose Club, no. 82, 1888

The Chase, plaster frieze
Exhibited Brasenose Club, no. 169, 1888

Gossip at the Well, bronze group three figures
Estate sale catalogue, no. 205

A Hunting Scene, wax model and coloured cast
Estate sale catalogue, no. 206

The Girl I Left Behind Me, wax model and plaster cast
Estate sale catalogue, no. 207

The Afghan War Medal, wax model
Done about 1881; dated from Harvard letters to engraver Leonard E.
Wyon, March 13 1881, in which Caldecott sketched details to be engraved

Crouching Cat, life-size terra-cotta statuette
Done about 1874, cf. Blackburn, *Randolph Caldecott,* 1886, p. 114;
original now owned by Victoria and Albert Museum

At Guingamp, Brittany, terra-cotta statuette
Done in 1874, reproduced in Blackburn, *Randolph Caldecott,* 1886, p.
113

A Pig of Brittany, terra-cotta statuette
Reproduced in Blackburn, *Randolph Caldecott,* 1886, p. 194

EXHIBITIONS:

CHESTER, CHESHIRE

1883   Caldecott donated several framed drawings and a painting,
        Frogs, for a charity exhibition organised by E. I. Baillie.

DUDLEY GALLERY

1872   Black and White Exhibition:
        Park Studies, no. 492, frame of 4 sepia ink drawings, priced
        5 gns.

        Cabinet Pictures in Oil:
        At the Coverside, no. 196, priced 10 gns.

1875   Black and White Exhibition:
        Breton Peasants, no. 235, sepia ink drawing, priced 5 gns.

        Doomed Lamb, no. 309, sepia ink drawing, priced 10 gns.

        Mare and Foal, no. 388, 10 gns.

FINE ART SOCIETY

1881   300 original drawings.

GROSVENOR GALLERY

1878   *The Boar Hunt,* no. 232, bronze bas-relief

1890   *The Last Flight,* no. 178, watercolour

        Hunting, no. 207, watercolour

HAMPSTEAD, LONDON

1885   Caldecott donated and had framed about 15 original drawings
        for a charity exhibition organised by a Mr. Gilchrist in
        Hampstead.

INSTITUTE OF PAINTERS IN WATER COLOUR

1883   *Putting the Hounds into Cover,* no. 817, reproduced *Academy
        Sketches,* 1883, p. 142

1885   *The First Flight,* no. 438, reproduced in *Academy Sketches,*
        1885, p. 135

MANCHESTER BRASENOSE CLUB

1888   Caldecott's old club held a posthumous memorial exhibition of
        173 ink drawings, water colour and oil paintings and sculpture at
        the club building.

MANCHESTER JUBILEE EXHIBITION

1887   *The Three Jolly Huntsmen,* bas-relief, no. 117

        The Girl I Left Behind Me, oil painting, no. 729

        May Day, oil painting, no. 738

        Meeting of Shareholders, oil painting, no. 739

        The Gardener's Little Daughter, oil painting, no. 847

PARIS SALON

1881   An exhibition of the works of Kate Greenaway, Walter Crane
        and Randolph Caldecott, described by J. K. Huysmans in *L'Art
        Moderne* (1883).

ROYAL ACADEMY

1876   *There were Three Ravens Sat on a Tree,* no. 415, oil painting

        Horse Fair in Brittany, no. 1499, metal bas-relief

1878   *The Three Huntsmen,* no. 597 with verse: 'So they Hunted and
        they hollo'd, Till the setting of the sun', oil painting

1882   *Scene from Spencer's 'Astrophel',* no. 1591, with verse: 'And
        many a nymph, both of the wood and brook, etc.', metal bas-
        relief

1906   *Hunting Scene,* no. 240, drawing

        Hunting Scene, no. 243, drawing

ROYAL MANCHESTER INSTITUTION

1869   *At the Wrong End of the Wood,* hunting frieze, white paint on
        brown paper, priced 10 gns.

1872   *Hunting Sketches*

1884   *May Day,* no. 798, oil painting

1886   *The Girl I Left Behind Me,* no. 747, oil painting

BIBLIOGRAPHY

Caldecott's Life and Work:

Anon, 'A Visit to Mr. Randolph Caldecott-I', *Pall Mall Gazette,* 4 January 1884; 'A Visit to Mr. Randolph Caldecott-II', *Pall Mall Gazette,* 7 January 1884; 'Souvenirs of Randolph Caldecott', *Pall Mall Gazette,* 11 June 1886
(Important contemporary accounts of his later life while in Kensington written by an anonymous journalist, with small sketches from his notebooks and 2 illustrated letters)

Henry Blackburn, *Randolph Caldecott,* London: Sampson Low, Marston, 1886
(Primary illustrated biography by a friend and patron which covers only early work until 1879)

J. Comyns Carr, 'La Royal Academy', *L'Art,* Vol. III, p. 211; Vol. IV, p. 18
(Series by editor of *The English Illustrated Magazine,* for which Caldecott provided illustrations, here mentions his work exhibited at the Royal Academy and illustrates 'The Three Jovial Huntsmen')

Catalogue of a Loan Collection of the Works of Randolph Caldecott exhibited at the Brasenose Club, Manchester, March 1888, Manchester: Private Press
(Largest exhibition of Caldecott's work, with introductory speeches by his brother, bank associates and dignitaries, and reproductions of little-known drawings)

Christie's Catalogue of the Whole of the Remaining Works of the Highly Talented Artist, Randolph Caldecott, London: 11 June 1886
(Estate sale catalogue with list of 218 items)

William Clough, *Randolph Caldecott,* London and Manchester, 1886.
(Reprinted newspaper article from the *Manchester Quarterly,* July 1886, by Caldecott's early bank associate and life-long friend)

Mary Gould Davis, *Randolph Caldecott. An Appreciation,* Philadelphia and New York: J. P. Lippincott, 1946
(Brief personal appraisal of his work with book list based on study of the Parker collection, Harvard University)

George Du Maurier, 'The Illustration of Books from a serious Artist's point of View—I, II', *Magazine of Art,* Vol. XII, 1890, pp. 349-353, 373-375
(Article by associate and friend assesses book illustration, mentions Caldecott's importance, illustrated with a family reading a Caldecott Picture Book)

Harry Furniss, *Confessions of a Caricaturist,* 2 volumes, London: T. Fisher & Unwin, 1901
(Autobiography of fellow illustrator for *Punch* with background on the duties of a reporter-illustrator)

Archibald S. Hartrick, *A Painter's Pilgrimage through Fifty Years,* Cambridge: University Press, 1939
(p. 33 mentions Caldecott's influence on Gauguin while at Pont Aven)

J. K. Huysmans, *L'Art Moderne,* Paris, 1883
(pp. 225-233 reviews Caldecott's work when exhibited with Kate Greenaway and Walter Crane at the Paris Salon of 1881)

L. M. Lamont, *Thomas Armstrong, C. B. A Memoir 1832-1911,* London: Martin Secker, 1912
(Describes Armstrong's friendship and relationship with Caldecott in the London of the 1870s)

Leslie Linder, *The Journal of Beatrix Potter from 1881-1897,* London and New York: Frederick Warne & Co., 1966
(Diary entry describes her father's purchase of Caldecott's work)

E. V. Lucas, *Edwin Austin Abbey. The Record of his Life and Work,* 2 volumes, London: Methuen & Co., New York: Charles Scribner & Sons, 1921
(Describes Abbey's friendship with Caldecott and admiration of his work; reproduction of illustrated letter between the two friends)

B. E. Mahony, L. P. Latimer, B. Folmsbee, *Illustrators of Children's Books 1744-1945,* Boston: Horn Books (reprint 1970)
(pp. 66-75 surveys Caldecott's work with 5 small illustrations)

Henry Stacy Marks, *Pen and Pencil Sketches,* 2 volumes, London: Chatto & Windus, 1894
(Autobiography by associate and decorative artist, with background on his London exhibitions)

Ruari McLean, *Reminiscences of Edmund Evans,* London: Oxford University Press, 1967
(Diaries of Caldecott's wood engraver with entries mentioning Caldecott; introduction, and book list of Evan's work)

Percy Muir, *Victorian Illustrated Books,* London: B. T. Batsford, 1971
(Thorough study of illustrators and publishers, with sections and book lists on Caldecott, Greenaway and Crane)

Leonée Ormand, *George Du Maurier,* London: Routledge & Kegan Paul, 1969
(Biography of Caldecott's friend and associate on *Punch* with references to their admiration for each other's works)

Joseph Pennell, *Pen Drawing and Pen Draughtsmanship. Their Work and their Methods,* London and New York: Macmillan & Co., 1889
(Written by the American illustrator as a practical treatise with chapter on Caldecott and English illustration and 5 line drawings)

Claude Phillips, 'Randolph Caldecott', *Gazette des Beaux Arts,* Vol. XXXIII, April 1886, pp. 327-341
(Most complete summary of Caldecott's work with 11 illustrations from the Picture Books)

M. H. Spielmann and Walter Jerrold, *Hugh Thomson. His Art. His Letters, His Humour and His Charm,* London: Adam and Charles Black, 1931
(Describes Thomson's early relationship with and life-long influence of Caldecott)

M. H. Spielmann and G. S. Layard, *Kate Greenaway,* London: Adam & Charles Black, 1905
(Mentions Kate Greenaway's admiration for Caldecott's work)

General material:

An Appendix to the Rowfant Library. A Catalogue of the Printed Books, Manuscripts, Autograph Letters, London: Chiswick Press, 1900

Laurence Binyon, *Catalogue of Drawings by British Artists in the British Museum,* 4 volumes, London: British Museum, 1898

Henry Blackburn, 'The Art of Popular Illustration', *Journal of the Society of Arts,* March 12 1875, pp. 367-375

Henry Blackburn, *The Art of Illustration,* London: W. H. Allen, 1894

Bryan's Dictionary of Painters and Engravers, 4 volumes, London: George Bell & Sons, 1904

Walter Crane, *Of the Decorative Illustration of Books Old and New,* London: George Bell & Sons [1896] (reprint 1972)

Rodney K. Engen, *Walter Crane as a Book Illustrator,* London: Academy Editions, 1975

Algernon Graves, *The Royal Academy of Arts, 1769-1904,* 8 volumes, Bath: Kingsmead, [1905] (reprint 1907)

Algernon Graves, *A Century of Loan Exhibitions 1813-1912,* 5 volumes, Bath: Kingsmead, [1913-15] (reprint 1971)

Martin Hardie, *English Coloured Books,* Bath: Kingsmead, [1906] (reprint 1973)

Estelle Jussim, *Visual Communication and the Graphic Arts,* London and New York: R. R. Bowker, 1975

Ruari MacLean, *Victorian Book Design and Colour Printing,* London: Faber & Faber, 1963

Iona and Peter Opie, *The Oxford Dictionary of Nursery Rhymes,* London: Oxford University Press, 1951

Forrest Reid, *Illustrators of the Eighteen Sixties,* New York: Dover, [1928] (reprint 1975)

R. Margaret Slythe, *The Art of Illustration 1750-1910,* London: Library Association, 1970

Isobel Spencer, *Walter Crane,* London: Studio Vista, 1976

James Thorpe, *English Illustration: the Nineties,* London: Faber & Faber, [1935] (reprint 1975)

Geoffrey Wakeman, *Victorian Book Illustration. The Technical Revolution,* Newton Abbot: David & Charles, 1973

Gleeson White, *English Illustration. 'The Sixties',* Bath: Kingsmead, [1897] (reprint 1970)

C. N. Williamson, 'Illustrated Journalism in England', *Magazine of Art',* Vol. XIII, 1890, pp. 334-40, 391-96

Christopher Wood, *Dictionary of Victorian Painters,* London: Antique Collector's Club, 1971